RAIL CENTRES:
BRISTOL

RAIL CENTRES:
BRISTOL

COLIN MAGGS

LONDON

IAN ALLAN LTD

First published 1981

ISBN 0 7110 1153 2

Published by Ian Allan Ltd, Shepperton, Surrey, and printed by Ian Allan Printing Ltd at their works at Coombelands in Runnymede, England.

Title page: Left:
Entrance to Temple Meads showing the effect with the central spire removed, 30 May 1980.   *Author*

Right: A view of Bath Road shed taken in August 1967 showing 'Hymeks', Class 47s, a Blue Pullman and one class 45.   *P. J. Fowler*

This page: No 5536 at Brislington with Bristol-Frome train. *R.J. Sellick*

Acknowledgements

Grateful acknowledgement for assistance is due to: M. J. Bishop; A. M. Child, Area Manager, Bristol and BR staff; J. Corin, Publicity Officer, Port of Bristol Authority; P. Davis who gave great assistance on Bristol locomotive builders and who is writing a book on the subject; B. Edwards; Mrs J. Gaskell; J. J. Herd; J. R. Robson; P. Smith; M. J. Tozer; J. W. P. Rowledge; and D. R. Steggles.

Contents

Outline History

For at least a thousand years there has been a settlement at Bristol. It developed at the confluence of the River Frome with the Bristol Avon at the lowest point where it was possible to bridge the latter and, indeed, the derivation of Bristol's name is from 'Brig-Stowe' meaning 'bridge-town'. For centuries Bristolians earned their living by trading or manufacturing – the Bristol Merchant Venturers being famous – and until a few years ago, ocean going vessels were able to moor at the city centre so that, when railways were invented, it was not surprising that they too converged on Bristol. As well as size making it a centre in its own right, the shape of the Severn estuary makes Bristol the natural gateway to the West of England from the Midlands and north, and the opening of the Severn Tunnel, made Bristol the gateway to Wales from the south coast and the west.

Although the Great Western Railway later became so important to the city, it was not the first railway to arrive. In the latter half of the 18th century Bristol required coal for its developing glass, pottery, sugar refining, brewing, distilling, soap making and smelting industries. Although some came from collieries near the city, more was readily available at Coalpit Heath, nine miles to the north, and early in the 19th century several abortive schemes were put forward to link these collieries with Bristol. The Bristol, Northern & Western Railway was a rather more grandiose scheme projected in 1824 to link Birmingham and Bristol, tapping the collieries at Coalpit Heath en route. Unfortunately the financial crisis of 1826 caused a large number of subscribers to call for the abandonment of the project, but they were not entirely successful and the Bristol & Gloucestershire Railway Act was passed on 19 June 1828. Although the line was to run only from Coalpit Heath to Bristol, its construction permitted doubling later should this have become necessary and it was anticipated that an extension would be built northwards.

The northern half of the line was opened in July 1832 as this was shared by the Avon & Gloucestershire Railway which had the rest of its line ready. The 515yd long Staple Hill Tunnel was eventually finished and the southern section of line ready for ceremonial opening on 6 August 1835. The horse drawn wagons were fitted with temporary seats to carry shareholders and friends and the nine miles to Coalpit Heath were covered in three hours. The party returned to Bristol together with 50 wagons carrying 200 tons of coal which reduced the price of this commodity at Bristol from 16 to 11 shillings per ton. The *Bristol Gazette* described the historic journey thus:

'The most interesting part of the journey was the descent of the inclined plane [the incline of 1 in 55 between Fishponds and Lawrence Hill] where the horses were removed and carriages impelled forward by force of gravitation. For some distance they proceeded at the rate of a quick trot, but so great was the command by which the guides (brakesmen) were possessed, by means of a lever acting upon the wheels, that though even here several stoppages took place, there was not the least danger of a collision.'

The Bristol terminus was at Cuckold's Pill (now Avonside Wharf) on the Floating Harbour opposite Temple Meads.

In 1839 the Bristol & Gloucester Railway, supported by the Great Western Railway (GWR) which had come into being four years previously, obtained an Act to absorb the Bristol & Gloucestershire. This Act also enabled them to extend the line to Standish and lay a third rail over the broad gauge Cheltenham & Great Western Union Railway to Gloucester where it would link with the narrow (standard) gauge Birmingham & Gloucester building a short connecting spur between Lawrence Hill and a junction with the GWR just outside the Bristol terminus. In 1841 contractors started work doubling the Bristol & Gloucestershire and building the extension. Two years later Brunel urged that the broad gauge be adopted as it offered several advantages: a joint station at Bristol would prove more convenient for passengers and Coalpit Heath coal could be taken to the industrial Stroud valley via the CGWUR, whereas competition would not have made transfer from trucks of one gauge to another economic; also a narrow gauge Bristol & Gloucester (BGR) in competition with the Great Western would have had traffic siphoned off by the GWR routing passengers and goods from Gloucester to Bristol via Swindon.

An arrangement was made with the GWR on 13 April 1843 which saved the BGR an outlay of £40-£50,000 and annual economies by the joint use of the GWR's passenger and goods stations at Bristol, Gloucester and Cheltenham, the only additional expense being the half mile of track from the BGR at Lawrence Hill to the GWR at Temple Meads. Powers for building this spur were granted on 27 June 1843. For £3,500 the BGR were able to enjoy at the three GWR stations 'the requisite accommodation for carriages and passengers, booking clerks, police and other assistants to attend to passengers

Right: **Rail routes to Bristol**

6

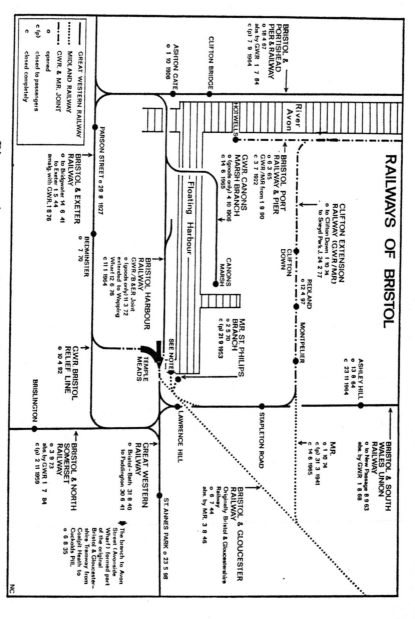

RAILWAYS OF BRISTOL

BRISTOL & PORTISHEAD PIER & RAILWAY
o 18.4.67
c (p) 7.9.1964
abs. by GWR 1.7.84

CLIFTON BRIDGE

ASHTON GATE
o 1.10.1906

CLIFTON EXTENSION RAILWAY (GWR/MR)
o to Clifton Down 1.10.74
to Sneyd Park J. 24.2.77

River Avon

HOTWELLS

BRISTOL PORT RAILWAY & PIER
o 6.3.65
GWR/MR from 1.9.90
c 3.7.1922

PARSON STREET o 29.8.1927

GWR. CANONS MARSH BRANCH
o (goods only) 4.10.1906
c 14.6.1965

BRISTOL & EXETER RAILWAY
o to Bridgwater 14.6.41
to Exeter 1.5.44
amalg. with GWR.1876

BEEMINSTER o 7.70

— Floating Harbour —

CANONS MARSH

BRISTOL HARBOUR RAILWAY
GWR/B&ER Joint
o (goods only) 11.3.72
extended to Wapping
Wharf 12.6.76
c 11.1964

CLIFTON DOWN

REDLAND o 12.4.97

MONTPELIER

MR. ST. PHILIPS BRANCH
o 2.5.70
c (p) 21.9.1953

SEE NOTE

TEMPLE MEADS

BRISLINGTON

GWR BRISTOL RELIEF LINE
o 10.4.92

BRISTOL & NORTH SOMERSET RAILWAY
o 3.9.73
abs. by GWR 1.7.84
c (p) 2.11.1959

ASHLEY HILL
o 13.8.64
c 23.11.1964

MR.
o 1.10.74
c (p) 31.3.1941
c 14.6.1965

STAPLETON ROAD

LAWRENCE HILL

ST ANNES PARK o 23.5.98

BRISTOL & SOUTH WALES UNION RAILWAY
o to New Passage 8.9.63
abs. by GWR 1.8.68

GREAT WESTERN RAILWAY
o Bristol-Bath 31.8.40
to Paddington 30.6.41

BRISTOL & GLOUCESTER RAILWAY
Originally Bristol & Gloucestershire Railway
o 6.7.44
abs. by MR. 3.8.46

The branch to Avon Street (Avonside Wharf) formed part of the original Bristol & Gloucestershire Tramway from Coalpit Heath to Cuckolds Pill
o 6.8.35

NC

Legend

———	GREAT WESTERN RAILWAY
— · — · —	MIDLAND RAILWAY
· · · · · · ·	GWR. & MR. JOINT
o	opened
c (p)	closed to passengers
c	closed completely

Diagrammatic representation of the railway network of Bristol

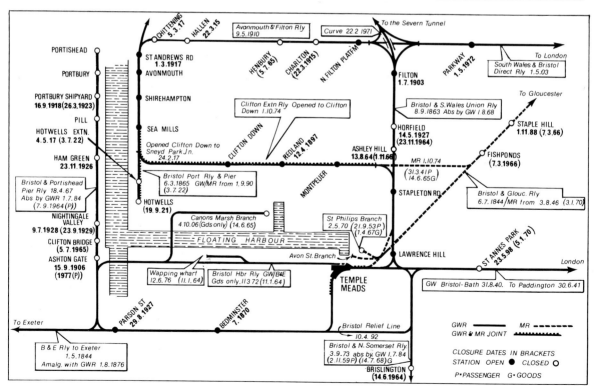

PASSENGERS MUST
CROSS THE LINE
BY THE BRIDGE

PORTISHEAD

PORTBURY

PORTBURY SHIPYARD
16.9.1918(26.3.1923)

PILL

HOTWELLS EXTN.
4.5.17 (3.7.22)

HAM GREEN
23.11.1926

*Bristol & Portishead
Pier Rly 18.4.67
Abs by GWR 1.7.84
(7.9.1964 (P))*

NIGHTINGALE
VALLEY
9.7.1928 (23.9.1929)

CLIFTON BRIDGE
(5.7.1965)

ASHTON GATE
15.9.1906
(1977 (P))

To Exeter

*B & E Rly to Exeter
1.5.1844
Amalg. with GWR 1.8.1876*

CHITTENING
5.3.17

HALLEN
22.3.15

*Avonmouth & Filton Rly
9.5.1910*

Curve 22.2.1971

To the Severn Tunnel

ST ANDREWS RD
1.3.1917
AVONMOUTH

HENBURY
(5.7.65)

CHARLTON
(22.3.1915)

N FILTON PLATFM.

FILTON
1.7.1903

PARKWAY
1.5.1972

To London

*South Wales & Bristol
Direct Rly 1.5.03*

SHIREHAMPTON

SEA MILLS

*Clifton Extn Rly Opened to Clifton
Down 1.10.74*

*Bristol & S.Wales Union Rly
8.9.1863 Abs by GW 1.8.68*

To Gloucester

HORFIELD
14.5.1927
(23.11.1964)

STAPLE HILL
1.11.88 (7.3.66)

*Opened Clifton Down to
Sneyd Park Jn.
24.2.17*

CLIFTON DOWN

REDLAND
12.4.1897

ASHLEY HILL
13.8.64 (1.11.66)

MR 1.10.74
(31.3.41 P)
(14.6.65 G)

FISHPONDS
(7.3.1966)

*Bristol Port Rly & Pier
6.3.1865 GW/MR from 1.9.90
(3.7.22)*

MONTPELIER

STAPLETON RD

*Bristol & Glouc. Rly
6.7.1844/MR from 3.8.46 (3.1.70)*

HOTWELLS
(19.9.21)

*Canons Marsh Branch
4.10.06 (Gds only) (14.6.65)*

*St Philips Branch
2.5.70 (21.9.53 P)
(1.4.67 G)*

FLOATING HARBOUR

Avon St.Branch

LAWRENCE HILL

ST ANNES PARK
23.5.98 (5.1.70)

London

*Wapping wharf
12.6.76 (11.1.64)*

*Bristol Hbr Rly GW/B&E
Gds only. 11.3 72 (11.1.64)*

TEMPLE
MEADS

GW Bristol-Bath 31.8.40. To Paddington 30.6.41

PARSON ST
29.8.1927

BEDMINSTER
7.1870

*Bristol Relief Line
10.4.92*

GWR ———— MR – – – –
GWR & MR JOINT ▬▬▬▬

*Bristol & N. Somerset Rly
3.9.73 abs by GW 1.7.84
(2.11.59 P) (14.7.68) G*

CLOSURE DATES IN BRACKETS
STATION OPEN ● CLOSED ○
P·PASSENGER G·GOODS

BRISLINGTON
(14.6.1964)

and their luggage' and also 'the necessary accommodation at the goods shed for merchandise traffic exclusive of minerals'.

As works were in quite an advanced state when the decision was made to change the gauge, the railway was never fully broad gauge width, Staple Hill Tunnel being only 26ft wide and underbridges the same. As GWR coaches were 11ft 5in wide over the lower footboards this gave a clearance of only about 10in between them and the tunnel wall and 18in between passing coaches. The line was opened on 8 July 1844 completing a chain of rail communications from Newcastle-on-Tyne to Exeter. On 14 January 1845 an agreement was signed by the Bristol & Gloucester and the Birmingham & Gloucester and both companies were worked as one until the Midland Railway took over on 7 May, its perpetual lease of the Bristol & Birmingham beginning on 1 July. The break of gauge at Gloucester was a hindrance and an Act of 14 August 1848 allowed the MR to mix the gauge from Bristol to Standish and build an independent narrow gauge line between there and Gloucester. MR narrow gauge trains first worked to Bristol on 29 May 1854, though a broad gauge Bristol & Exeter train continued to

run over the line to Parkfield Colliery just south of Westerleigh, until January 1882.

The second railway to enter Bristol was the GWR. Back in the 1820s Bristol was the second city in the kingdom and it was not surprising that plans were put forward to make a rail link with the capital. The first proposal was the London & Bristol Rail-Road Company, promoted by Bristol merchants in 1824. Encouraged by the successful opening of the Stockton & Darlington Railway in 1825, Bristolians devised similar schemes but none reached the practical stage. In the autumn of 1832, four Bristolians met in Temple Back, later covered by Temple Meads goods depot, and formed a committee which included representatives of the Society of Merchant Venturers and the Bristol & Gloucestershire Railway which had opened its line from Coalpit Heath to Mangotsfield, but was yet to reach Bristol. The committee advertised for an engineer and the young Isambard Kingdom Brunel was appointed on 7 March 1833. The outcome of a public meeting held in Bristol on 30 July 1833 to consider Brunel's report, was the passing of a resolution for the formation of a company which became the Great Western Railway, its bill receiving Royal Assent 31 August 1835. No time was wasted and the first stage of the railway between Bristol and Bath was begun the following month and during the autumn and winter most of the land was bought. The GWR had hoped to open the line in the spring of 1838, but the contractor fell into financial difficulty. The GWR seized his work, Ranger responding by taking legal proceedings and engaging in a long and expensive lawsuit which was not settled until it

Left: **Staple Hill station and tunnel, 21 April 1960.** *Author*

Below left: **Diagrammatic representation of the railway history of Bristol**

Below: **Bridge over the Avon west of East Depot.** *J.C. Bourne*

Above: Brunel's train shed.   *J.C. Bourne*

Above right: Map of the Bristol area

Right: Map of the Bristol area – enlargement of central area

reached the House of Lords in 1847. Meanwhile, by August 1839 most of the work on the line to Bath was complete except for the bridge over the Floating Harbour immediately east of Bristol station where difficulty was experienced with Ranger's poor foundations.

The Bristol Board of Great Western directors, working independently of those in London, announced that the Bristol to Bath line would open on 31 August 1840. A few minutes before 8am the train of three first class and five second class coaches was nearly full. Just after the hour the bell was rung and *Fire Ball* left, less than half an hour after the last rail had been laid. Some 5,880 passengers were carried on the first day in 10 trains each way and £476 was taken, comparing favourably with £226 when the line was opened from Paddington to Maidenhead two years earlier.

In its opening week the railway played its part in apprehending a criminal. A gentleman from Bath arriving at Bristol found that he had been robbed of £120. Suspecting a man who had boarded the up train which had already departed, he reported the theft to the railway authorities who for safety strapped him to a light engine. It took him to Bath on the *down* line in 11½ minutes (an average speed of 60mph) and arrived before the train from Bristol in which the thief was travelling. The Bath police were informed and the surprised robber arrested as he left the train.

The section through Box Tunnel being completed, the GWR was opened throughout from London to Bristol on 30 June 1841, a beflagged train with directors on board leaving Paddington at 8am and arriving at Bristol at noon. However the importance of the occasion was belittled by the *Bristol Mercury* which was so full of jubilation over the victory of the Liberal candidate in the General Election, that it merely commented: 'Several trains passed over the line to and from London during the day. We have not heard of any accident occurring on the occasion, except that an engine which propelled the down train from town got off the rails near the station.'

A month after the Act of Parliament had been passed authorising the GWR to build a line from London, Bristol merchants issued a prospectus for an extension of the broad gauge to Exeter. Apart from opening up a railway to the west, the line also had the attraction of tapping a 'vast coalfield' to the west of Bristol at Backwell and Nailsea and of running close to the natural harbour of Uphill near Weston super Mare, though in the event, neither of these allurements brought the company much dividend.

Things moved very rapidly. Within a month the estimated capital of £1.5million had been subscribed, a survey made and the necessary plans deposited. Of the

10

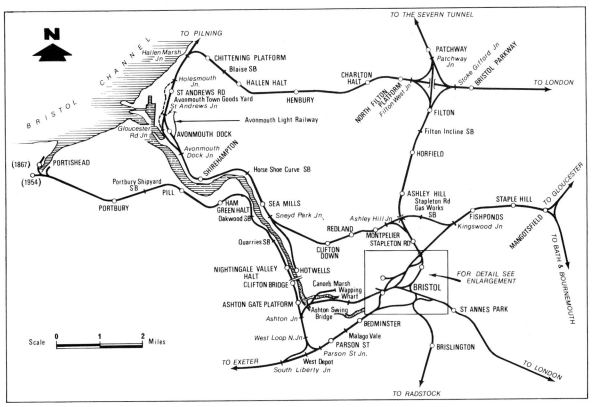

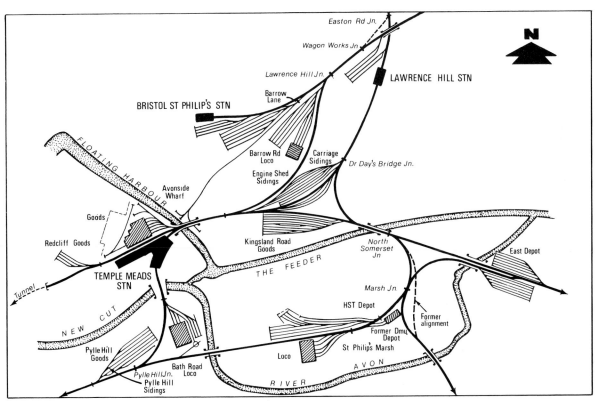

11

16 directors, 12 were Bristolians and none were directors of the GWR, though the two companies shared the same engineer, I. K. Brunel, his assistant William Gravatt undertaking much of the work. Gravatt had worked with Marc and Isambard Brunel on the Thames Tunnel at Rotherhithe, but on the B&E Gravatt proved unsatisfactory and let down his chief. Brunel censured him for 'a most unprofessional act sacrificing your duty to the Company, to me and to yourself', and on 23 July 1840 Brunel wrote a letter to him with the first two words of 'My dear Garratt' deleted. On 4 June 1841 Brunel wrote to Garratt regarding the B&E bridge south of Bristol station 'How could you leave me uninformed of the deplorable state of the bridge near the New Cut?' and 10 days later asked him to resign. Gravatt refused and made countercharges, but the directors upheld Brunel.

Work had begun at the Bristol end of the line in February 1837, the chief engineering features being a 120ft masonry bridge across the New Cut and a cutting through the shoulder of Pylle Hill. In 1839 the plan of having a temporary terminus at Pylle Hill was abandoned and it was decided to build a station adjoining that of the GWR. The B&E wanted to save capital by not buying locomotives and rolling stock because of non-payments of calls on its shares (the third call did not produce more than £1,000 and B&E shares on which £5 had been paid

were selling for 2s 6d), and so in 1840 it persuaded the GWR to lease the line to Bridgwater for an annual rental of £30,000 and a toll of a farthing a mile on every passenger and ton of goods carried. Using existing local talent, Messrs T. J. & J. F. Perry, road carriage builders of Bristol, constructed two first class coaches for use on the line.

On 1 June 1841 thousands gathered at Bristol to see *Fire Ball*, once again selected to work an initial train, leave the temporary wooden station with a train of eight coaches containing 400 passengers. As a consequence of being delayed 46 minutes at Bristol, the engine ran short of water and had to stop at Nailsea to replenish its tender. The line opened to the public on 14 June when fares taken amounted to £302. The line was opened to Exeter on 1 May 1844 giving the GWR a main line 194 miles in length – the longest in the kingdom. The B&E was eventually absorbed by the GWR on 1 August 1876, a year after mixed gauge had been opened between Bristol and Taunton, mixed gauge arriving at Bristol from the east in 1874. There had been a chance that the B&E might have been taken over by the Midland Railway but for the fact that Derby at that time was committed to building the very expensive Settle & Carlisle line.

The last of the main line railways to Bristol was the Bristol & South Wales Union Railway. As the crow flies, Bristol is only 25 miles from Cardiff, but just over a century ago, the fastest way to travel between the two cities was to travel by rail via Gloucester, a distance no less than 93 miles! A short cut was obviously needed. The first attempt at this was in April 1845 when the Bristol &

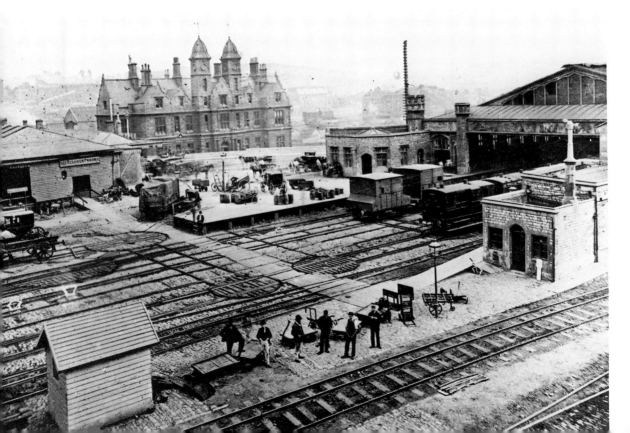

South Wales Junction Railway was mooted. 18 months later, its promoters bought the rights of the Old and New Passage Ferries across the Severn, but the company was wound up in 1853. The fact that Old Passage Ferry cost the company £30,000 is indicative of its importance as a route. The following year a proposal was made to build a line from Bristol via Hotwells, Shirehampton and New Passage where it was to cross the Severn by means of a floating bridge. That idea too was abortive, but the third attempt, the BSWUR, succeeded. Parliament passed the necessary Act on 27 July 1857 granting powers for a railway between South Wales Junction, half a mile east of Temple Meads, and New Passage Pier, where a ferry ran across two miles of water to Portskewett Pier, a branch connecting with the South Wales Railway. Brunel was appointed engineer, though his health was failing by this time and he was succeeded by R. P. Brereton, with Charles Richardson as resident engineer. The works begun in October 1858 included a heavy cutting at Horfield and the 11½ miles of single line were constructed to the broad gauge. Rowland Brotherhood of Chippenham was the contractor and to carry out his various works he required locomotives; in the days of horse drawn wagons and poor roads, it was difficult moving engines from one part of the country to another. To ease this problem Rowland's son, Peter, designed an engine capable of travelling on road or railway and in 1862 one of these 11ton machines travelled from Chippenham via Acton Turville and Iron Acton to the BSWUR at Patchway over ordinary roads at an average speed of 6mph.

In 1859 the two ferries were again bought. Richardson planned the piers so that trains could run to their ends and steamers land passengers at any state of the tide. It was while engaged on building these jetties that he was led to consider the project of cutting a tunnel under the Severn. The BSWUR was opened ceremonially on 25 August 1863 and to the public on 8 September. It was Bristol's first suburban railway and had stations at Lawrence Hill, Stapleton Road and Filton, Ashley Hill being opened the following year and Horfield in 1927. There was a two-mile bank of 1 in 75 between Stapleton Road and Horfield.

As was usual with relatively minor railways, the company did not own locomotives and rolling stock, but had its line worked by a larger company, in this case the GWR. The first Sunday excursion over the line was run on 13 September 1863 when more than 1,500 passengers were carried in a train of 21 coaches. On the return journey, the train stalled in Patchway Tunnel because it was overloaded.

The BSWUR was converted to narrow gauge 7-9 August 1873. 33 hours were allotted for the task of converting the 11.5 miles, but it was completed within 28 hours. Men engaged on the work were allowed to take the usual mealtimes, each gang of 20 having one man to cook their food. The railway company banned alcohol

Below: **Stapleton Road station c1900.** *Author's collection*

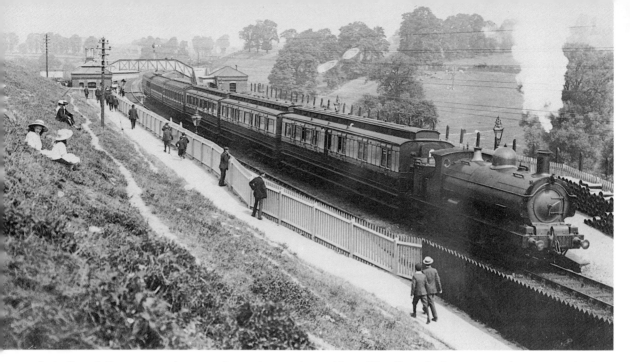

but allowed them as much oatmeal porridge as they could drink. Although the opening of the BSWUR eased travel between South Wales and Bristol, it was far from ideal as the change from train to ship was inconvenient for passengers and not feasible for goods. The GWR proposed replacing the ferry by a 4.5-mile tunnel and on 18 March 1873 work started, a task fraught with difficulties and dangers. To cope with the expected increase of traffic on the BSWUR when the Severn Tunnel was opened, Narroways Hill Junction to Patchway was doubled by a new up line being built and first used on 1 September 1886, the day the tunnel was opened to goods traffic. Passenger traffic began on 1 December, turning what had been a branch into an important trunk route. To give a direct run from London to South Wales through the Severn Tunnel, in September 1886 an important 26-chain curve was opened from North Somerset Junction to Dr Day's Bridge Junction. From July 1887 main passenger services from London to South Wales were diverted from the Gloucester route to run via Bath and the new spur. The increase in the number of trains between Dr Day's Bridge Junction and Narroways Hill Junction where Avonmouth trains diverged, led to its quadrupling in November 1891.

Bristol was now an important rail centre, with main lines to London, Cardiff, Birmingham and Exeter. Added to this, all of the London-Exeter and London-South Wales traffic had to pass through the city until the opening of two cutoffs – the South Wales & Bristol Direct line on 1 May 1903 and the Castle Cary-Cogload Junction line on 11 June 1906. However, the GWR had to face considerable competition because of the site of Temple Meads (three-quarters of a mile from the city centre) and because of its roundabout routes to the West Country, which led to the play on the GWR's initials – the

'Great Way Round'. Competition also came in the form of several schemes for alternative London-Bristol routes – one of which was the Bristol & London & South Western Junction Railway, a scheme launched in Bristol. The plan (deposited in 1882) was for a line from the London & South Western Railway near Grateley, west of Andover, to Radstock where it should have connected with both the Bristol & North Somerset Railway and the Somerset & Dorset Joint Railway. The BNSR would have been doubled and a new line built from immediately north of its bridge over the Avon to a terminus close to the Centre. The distance of this line from Bristol to Waterloo would have compared favourable with the GWR's route, being only a few miles longer – about 130 compared to 118 miles.

It was by no means the first mooting of the scheme. In 1834 the London & Southampton Railway had planned a branch from Basingstoke to Bristol, while in 1862 the Bristol & South Western Junction Railway was promoted for linking the LSWR at Gillingham with Bristol. Attempts had also been made to solve the problem of Temple Meads' position on the outskirts of the city. In 1861 the Bristol & Clifton Railway had proposed a line from Temple Meads to a central station at Queen Square, with an extension to a terminus on Brandon Hill.

In January 1883 the provisional committee, including 150 Bristol merchants, traders and manufacturers disgruntled by the GWR service, discovered the LSWR would not support the bill unless the MR was in favour. This was not the case, the Midland petitioning against it believing that a new line would siphon traffic from its line, rather than bring additional traffic. In order to gain MR and LSWR support, the bill was amended to provide a railway from Grateley to the S&D at Wellow north of Radstock, trains to Bristol proceeding over the S&D and MR. It was planned that the LSWR would work trains

Above left: **0-6-0ST No 1874 leaving Ashley Hill with train for Temple Meads, c1900.** *Author's collection*

Above: **No 7029** *Clun Castle* **travelling east to north at Dr Day's Bridge Junction with LCGB special, 6 February 1965.** *H. Ballantyne*

from Waterloo to Bath and the MR from Bath to Bristol. This was because the terminal layout at Bath Green Park made reversal and engine changing necessary and also the fact that the MR already possessed running powers into Temple Meads whereas the GWR would have strongly opposed any such powers being granted to the LSWR. The abandonment of a central station at Bristol saved £600,000 and the mileage from Waterloo was increased to 133½.

The GWR opposing the bill anticipated it would lose some third class passenger traffic to London, a proportion of the goods traffic, the combined total amounting to some £20,000-£30,000 annually. The House of Commons Committee rejected the bill. Although the promoters hoped to present a further scheme the following year, they did not in fact do so because of a peace agreement made between the GWR and LSWR in October 1884.

Charles Wills, a leading spirit behind the Bristol docks expansion scheme of the 1870s, continued to put forward alternatives to the GWR line to London, his most ambitious being the Bristol, London & Southern Counties Railway, the order of these places being significant. The line was to run from a station at the Centre, parallel to the GWR through Bath, Bradford on Avon and Trowbridge where it would have struck across country to a junction with the LSWR at Overton east of

Basingstoke. This route to Waterloo would have been only seven chains more than the route to Paddington. A branch would have run to Avonmouth where work had started on the Royal Edward Dock. In addition to the station at the Centre, the line would have provided the much needed rail access to the deep water berths at Canon's Marsh. In order to save valuable space the station at Bristol would have been of double deck construction with passenger accommodation above and the goods depot below. In June 1903 the House of Commons Committee declared that the preamble to the bill had not been proved and in spite of the Bristol Corporation voting £100,000 for investment in shares, the Committee was unconvinced that the required capital of £5million could be raised.

The South Wales & Bristol Direct Railway was built as a result of people in South Wales being very dissatisfied with the GWR service and threatening to build an entirely new line from Cardiff to the LSWR near Grateley. The 31-mile long SWBDR had several advantages: it shortened the distance from London to South Wales by 10 miles; enabled the 1 in 75 incline to Horfield to be avoided; shortened the distance from London to Bristol by a mile and relieved the busy Bristol-Bathampton line of London-South Wales traffic, this section not being easily quadrupled because of the heavy engineering works required. The first through goods to use the SWBDR was on 1 May 1903 and the initial passenger train on 1 July. In contrast to the impressive ceremonies of the Victorian era, the first train merely carried the Superintendent of the Bristol Division of the GWR and several company officials. On 30 April 1933 the quadrupled tracks from Filton Junction-Stapleton Road were opened, two new main tracks having been laid east of the original lines which became the relief.

The first of the branch lines, and the first line built as

standard gauge radiating from Bristol, was the Bristol Port Railway & Pier. During the 19th century the size of vessels had increased to such an extent that some ships had too great a draught to navigate the Avon to Bristol safely. The BPRP and the Bristol Port & Channel Dock companies were formed in 1862 and 1864 respectively with almost identical promoters. On 17 July 1862 the BPRP received its Act to build a 5.75-mile long single standard gauge line from a terminus at Hotwells to Avonmouth. As it was not proposed to cater for anything other than purely local traffic, no connection with any other railway was thought necessary. Benjamin Burleigh was appointed engineer. The precise opening date of 6 March 1865 was purposely withheld so that the line would not be overwhelmed by vast crowds that the single

Top: **25 locomotives used on John Aird's Royal Edward Dock contract at Avonmouth.** *J. Walford collection*

Above: **Ashley Hill station after quadrupling.** *BR*

Right: **GWR 0-4-2T with train of five coaches at Hotwells c1895. Platform road has inside key track.** *R. Hack collection*

engine could not handle, and timetables were only posted up outside Hotwells station a few minutes before the departure of the first train. The BPRP, with virtually no goods traffic, realised that if it hoped to build a commercially viable dock at Avonmouth, through rail communication with other railways was essential. Since a

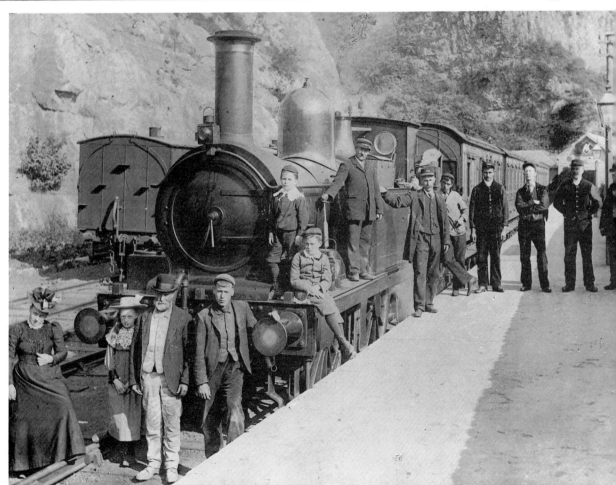

line from Hotwells to Temple Meads over developed land would have cost £700,000, a scheme for a line at only about a quarter of this cost was proposed from the BPRP at Sneyd Park to the BSWUR and the MR. As the financial position of the BPRP was too poor to attract investors, a separate company was floated. The double track Clifton Extension Railway received its Act on 15 August 1867 and was managed by a committee formed of two representatives from each of the BPRP, GWR and MR, the latter two companies providing the finance. The greatest engineering feature of the CER was Clifton Down Tunnel. Colonel Yolland's inspection train on 15 June 1874 was drawn by four locomotives – two GWR and two MR. The line opened for passenger traffic to Clifton Down on 1 October, all trains being well-patronised and pick-pockets plying their trade on the crowded platforms.

On 16 March 1875 the Mayor of Bristol inspected Clifton Down Tunnel. Two horses drew a contractor's wagon into it with his party aboard, where, according to the *Western Daily Press*, 'the visitors met with a very cool reception'. Although the tunnel was finished in May, the Board of Trade inspector would not pass Sneyd Park Junction to passenger traffic because he believed that the 150ft length platform of Sea Mills station was inadequate. The contested decision was upheld. With the opening of Avonmouth Docks on 24 February 1877, goods trains began working through the tunnel and the platform at Sea Mills was lengthened at the BPRP's expense. On 3 August 1878 Col Yolland, the Board of Trade inspector, sanctioned the opening of Clifton Down-Sneyd Park Junction to passenger trains, though in fact none ran because the GWR and MR felt that the BPRP line was not in a satisfactory condition to carry them. The Midland obtained Parliamentary powers to install block signalling and charge the expense to the BPRP and eventually the line was opened to passengers on 1 September 1885. The single line beyond Sneyd Park was quite inadequate to cope with increasing traffic to and from Avonmouth, so Avonmouth Dock-Shirehampton was doubled 16 May 1903 and Shirehampton-Sneyd Park Junction on 6 January 1907. After World War I Bristol Corporation decided to build a direct road to Avonmouth through the Avon Gorge to avoid the route over the Downs. As there was insufficient room for both road and railway, it obtained an Act on 16 August 1920 for taking over the line from Hotwells to Sneyd Park Junction, which closed 3 July 1922. With the reduction in freight services, traffic was light enough for the economy to be made of singling the line from Ashley Hill Junction to Avonmouth on 19 October 1970.

The first proposal for a line to Portishead was made as early as 1800. A Mr Grace, colliery owner of Bristol, proposed building a railway from his pits to his wharf at Portishead. He planned it on a gradient in order that the descending loaded wagons could draw up the empties, but this interesting project was dropped. In 1845 Brunel proposed building a floating pier at Portbury and linking it to Bristol by means of an atmospheric railway. The Portbury Pier & Railway Co obtained its Act on 3 August

Above: **Clifton Down, view towards Avonmouth.** *Lens of Sutton*

Left: Portishead line under construction c1866 near site of Clifton Bridge station.   *Bristol Museum*

Below: Down train hauled by a 2-2-2 WT at Clifton Bridge c1867.   *M.J. Tozer collection*

Bottom: B&E 4-4-0ST No 72 with up train at Portishead c1870.   *Bristol Museum*

1846 but was wound up five years later, a victim of the lean years following the 'Railway Mania'. The district was determined not to be left off the railway map so in 1863 the Bristol & Portishead Pier & Railway Co obtained Parliamentary powers to build a line from the B&E at Bedminster to a pier at Portbury, with a minor branch running to the village of Portishead. A change of plan caused the company to abandon the Portbury terminus and make Portishead the main line. The 9½-mile single broad gauge branch was opened 18 April 1867 and worked by the B&E. The pier opened in June 1868 and was extended 300ft two years later so that vessels could use it at low water. The company was enterprising enough to operate steamers to Newport and Cardiff all the year round (the Severn Tunnel was not yet opened) and a special service to Ilfracombe in the summer with through rail and steamer bookings from the GWR and MR, passengers travelling to a special pier platform beyond the town station.

In 1871 a bill was promoted to turn Portishead Pill into a dock. As the BPRP on the opposite bank also had dock plans before Parliament that year, both were competing for a subscription of £100,000 from Bristol Corporation. The GWR, as successors of the B&E, bought the railway and pier in 1884, the dock being sold to Bristol Corporation, the line having been narrowed 24-27 January 1880. Portishead power station was enlarged after World War 2, the electricity authority taking over the site of the railway station. This necessitated the building of a new station in 1954 at a cost of £250,000, and it had the honour of being the first such new building since the war. The branch closed to passenger traffic on 7 September 1964.

The first railway to reach Radstock was a branch of the broad gauge Wilts, Somerset & Weymouth Railway from Frome, which tapped lucrative coal traffic. Having thus projected a line into a mining area, it was thought profitable to continue it northwards to link with the main

GWR line at Keynsham or Bristol, tapping further collieries en route. In 1862 plans for the Bristol & North Somerset Railway were drawn up. The line was to run from Bristol, through Pensford, Clutton, Hallatrow and Midsomer Norton to Radstock, then climbing over the Mendips on long gradients of 1 in 50, down to Shepton Mallet and on to a junction near Bruton with the Somerset Central Railway. This railway was one of the constituent companies of the Somerset & Dorset Railway whose Bath Extension had yet to be built. By an Act of 21 July 1863 the BNSR was incorporated to make railways connecting the MR, GWR and S&D, the backbone of the scheme being the standard gauge Bristol-Radstock line. The first turf was turned on 7 October 1873 at the mining village of Clutton, but financial difficulties beset the company, land was not purchased and the contractor was forced to stop work. A second contractor came on the scene and works were continued a little further, only to be suspended again. Between 1864 and 1866 the S&D tried unsuccessfully to woo the BNSR. Both railways had their monetary problems and in 1866 the BNSR made an agreement with the GWR. On 23 July 1866 a further Act was passed for raising additional capital and on 31 July 1868 an extension of time was granted, as were powers for several deviations. The credit of the company was not improved when its secretary, John Bingham, who had run up huge bills for legal and Parliamentary expenses, was sentenced in June 1870 to

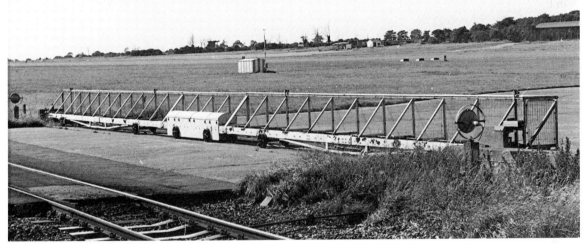

12 months' imprisonment with hard labour for attempting to defraud W. M. Baillie, the company's Bristol banker and largest shareholder, Bingham had forged an endorsement on a draft of £536.

A new company was formed in the latter part of 1870, BNSR creditors receiving shares at par in lieu of their debts. A third contractor completed the railway and the GWR undertook to work the finished line which was opened throughout on 3 September 1873, creating a break of gauge at Radstock until the Radstock-Frome branch was narrowed the following June. The GWR absorbed the BNSR on 1 July 1884, partly on economic grounds as the line tapping the coalfield had a considerable potential, while an additional factor for purchase was to prevent it falling into the hands of the MR or LSWR. The branch closed to passengers on 2 November 1959 and following a landslip caused by a heavy storm, was closed completely from Midsomer Norton to Marsh Junction on 14 July 1968.

When the direct line between Wootton Bassett and Patchway was opened in 1903, the need was felt for a straight route to and from Avonmouth docks, so on 9 May 1910 a 6.75-mile long single line was opened from Filton and Stoke Gifford to Holesmouth Junction, Avonmouth, avoiding the use of the heavily graded Clifton Down line. The main feature of the Henbury line was the 302yd Charlton Tunnel. As well as being useful for goods traffic, the new line provided rail communication for villages north of Bristol until 30 April 1915 when the railmotor was withdrawn and the halts closed.

Chittening Platform with its austere corrugated asbestos shelters was built during World War 1 to serve what would have been the second largest government factory in the country. By May 1917 the whole branch was doubled to cope with the expected traffic, but the entry of the USA into the war caused the British government to abandon the project.

After World War 2 the Bristol Aeroplane Company at Filton developed the large 'Brabazon' and between 13 October and 10 November 1947, temporary single line working was instituted between Henbury and Filton West to allow the installation of an aircraft level crossing over the railway in order to give access from the building hangar to a new runway long enough to allow the aircraft to take off. When BAC wished to take aircraft over the crossing they rang Filton West signalbox and, if the line was clear, a release was given to the motors operating the sliding gates. After the passage of an aircraft BAC restored the gates to normal and, providing a proving circuit was made, normal train operation continued. Today the telephone is connected to the Bristol Panel Box. The branch was closed to passenger traffic from 23 November 1964 and singled on 22 May 1966. During World War 1 earthworks were made for a curve from Filton West Junction to Patchway, but no track was laid. However to facilitate traffic to and from South Wales, particularly zoo excursions to Clifton Down, the curve was opened on 22 February 1971. North Filton platform is still used by one train morning and afternoon for BAC workers, but does not appear in the public timetable.

To ease the situation at Temple Meads which was becoming very crowded, an avoiding line from Pylle Hill through St Philip's Marsh to North Somerset Junction was opened on 10 April 1892, though because of falling traffic, it was found that the western half could be singled on 19 April 1970. Despite the curtailment of Britain's railway system, Bristol has remained an important rail centre because it is still an exchange point between main lines from London, South Wales, Portsmouth, Weymouth, the midlands and the south-west and in addition has a large hinterland which generates considerable traffic.

Top: **Set No 462 at North Filton Platform working the 16.45 to Temple Meads on 21 August 1980.**   *Author*

Above: **Pylle Hill Junction, view towards Bath Road depot, September 1932.**   *H.C. Leat, Bristol Photographic Society per M.J. Tozer*

Below: **Bath Road MPD, turntable and Bristol Avoiding Line, 18 August 1980.**   *Author*

Development of Passenger Working

In 1840 the first train service from Bristol to Bath gave 10 each way daily taking 25 minutes for the 11.75 miles including a stop at Keynsham. These ran in competition with 70 road coaches and soon put them off the highway. In December when stations opened at Saltford and Twerton an extra train was added each way, but third class traffic and goods were not carried until the opening of the line from London on 30 June 1841. The down night mail was the fastest train covering the 118½ miles in 4hr 10min with 10 stops, but third class passengers travelling by goods train took 9½hr. In 1845 the forerunner of the 'Flying Dutchman' ran to Bristol in 3hr and on to Exeter in another 2hr. In 1848 it was speeded to 2½hr to Bristol including the 10min refreshment stop at Swindon. The GWR was early in the excursion field and ran a trip from Bristol to London at 21 shillings (£1.05), half the normal rate, on 29 September 1842, the train of 700-800 passengers being drawn by two locomotives. One interesting service from Temple Meads only lasting for five months in 1864 involved slipping a coach at West London Junction for Kensington and Victoria.

A note in the early timetables stated that 'London time is kept at all stations on the railway, which is about 11 minutes before Bristol and Bath time, and 14 minutes before Bridgwater time.' Because of the inconvenience of local time being different from railway time, Greenwich time was adopted at Bristol on 14 September 1852, but only after a prolonged struggle on behalf of local custom. Bristol was one of the first cities to issue local railway guides. The *Bristol Steam Packet and Railway Monthly Timetable and Family Calendar* was published in January 1853 and was followed in July 1854 by a rival publication wishing to cash in on its success.

In view of the looming threat of the Bristol & London & South Western Junction Railway, in June 1882 GWR express fares were abolished and all trains except two expresses each way carried third class passengers. In April 1883 11 through passenger trains ran to London compared with nine in 1862, while in July 1883 a new fast train left Bristol at 9.35am and reached Paddington in 2hr 50min, one in the other direction leaving at 6.20pm

Below: No 7024 *Powis Castle* at Platform 5 with the last down steam hauled 'Bristolian' on 12 June 1959. Platform clock read 10.26 and the train was not due in until 10.30. *H. Ballantyne*

Left: No 5085 *Evesham Abbey* at Platform 9 waiting to leave with the last steam hauled up 'Bristolian', 12 June 1959. *H. Ballantyne*

Centre left: No 7019 *Fowey Castle* roars through Filton Junction station with the up 'Bristolian', 19 May 1959. *H. Ballantyne*

Below: Another named train from Paddington-Bristol was the 'Merchant Venturer'. No 4967 *Shirenewton Hall* stands at the head of the 'Merchant Venturer' ready to take it on to Weston super Mare, No 6009 *King Charles II* having hauled the train from Paddington. *R.E. Toop*

Below right: No 6019 *King Henry V* with the 9.5am ex-Paddington arriving at Temple Meads, 12 June 1959. *H. Ballantyne*

and arriving at Bristol in 2hr 55min, this being a direct result of complaints of Bristol witnesses before the House of Commons Committee looking into the BLSWJR bill. In the spring of 1884 a sleeping car service was introduced for first class passengers.

The last public up broad gauge train from Bristol was the mail which departed at 12.45am on 21 May 1892 hauled by *Bulkeley*. Thirteen special trains taking broad gauge rolling stock from Devon and Cornwall passed Bristol during the night en route for Swindon, while additionally some broad gauge coaches were placed in sidings at Exeter to be taken to Swindon later as the mixed gauge east of Exeter was not immediately removed. Following the abolition of the compulsory refreshment stop at Swindon the 'Cornishman' ran non-stop Paddington to Bristol in 2¼hr while on 28 July 1896 the longest non-stop run in the world was inaugurated when the first portion of the 'Cornishman' ran to Exeter in 3¾hr via the Bristol relief line, while the same year restaurant cars were introduced for first class passengers. From 1 July 1903 the service was speeded by 15min, on which date the *City of Bath* arrived at Temple Meads 4min early. To mark the centenary of the opening of the Great Western, on 9 September 1935 the 'Bristolian' was timed to reach Temple Meads in 1¾hr – 15 minutes better than the previous best and giving an average speed of 67.6mph and 67.2mph up. A 'King' was used for the first few months, but subsequently it was hauled by a 'Castle'. With the introduction of 'Warships' in 1959 it was speeded up to 1hr 40min but for the winter

of 1959 the Civil Engineer ensured that it was put back to the original timing of 1¾hr in order that 'Warships' could be limited to 90mph. In 1961 when an even interval timetable was introduced it called at Bath and to enable its loading to be increased to 10 or 11 coaches, the allowance was increased to 1hr 54min.

In 1960 the diesel 'Bristol Pullman' was introduced, but its Swiss-designed Schlieren bogie failed to give the shorter British bodies a good ride. It left Temple Meads at 07.45 non stop via Badminton; then returned at midday from London calling at Bath and finally ran the 16.55 Paddington to Bristol non-stop via Badminton, the 110min runs being slower than the 'Bristolian'. From October 1960 it was re-routed morning and evening via Bath. In 1968 it was speeded up to 100min including a stop at Bath, but decelerated by 5min in 1972 when a Chippenham stop was inserted into the up morning and down evening trip. The WR had three 8-car two class units and the LMR two 6-car one class units used between St Pancras and Manchester until electrification. In March 1967 the two LMR units were modified for multiple unit operation and two class accommodation and put into a 12-car formation for the up run from Bristol and then divided for the midday return run: one to Bristol and one to Oxford, uniting again for the evening run from Paddington to Bristol, but the midday services were poorly patronised and ceased in 1969. The introduction of air conditioned and better riding Mk II coaches caused the Blue Pullmans to have little appeal and they were taken out of service in the spring of 1973.

Left: 08.20 up 'Bristol Pullman' on 5 June 1958. *Author*

Right: No 253.001 at Temple Meads with the 17.10 to Paddington on 1 August 1980. *Author*

Below: No 5609, then unnamed, with the up 'Devonian' at Temple Meads in 1937. *NRM*

Pre-production HST No 252.001 ran various trains from Bristol at conventional speeds from 1975. HSTs were introduced 4 October 1976, five each way knocking 22min off the time to Parkway and 15min off the time to Temple Meads. Four trains were in service with one as standby and one for crew training. A full service of hourly trains from Bristol to Paddington began in the spring of 1977, the fastest covering the distance in 1hr 30min.

The opening of the South Wales & Bristol Direct line on 1 July 1903 meant that trains for the Principality could avoid Bristol and four new direct expresses were run over the new line to South Wales. There were now three routes from Bristol to London: via Badminton, Chippenham or Devizes. In 1927 two slip coaches for Bristol were detached from South Wales expresses at Stoke Gifford. On 1 July 1908 an express was introduced from Penzance to Wolverhampton which ran through Bristol, and the following summer a Bristol-Birkenhead and a Weston super Mare-Wolverhampton were added. That same year (1909) the GWR stirred things by retiming an up express from the West Country to miss a connection with the MR 4.40pm to Birmingham by 4min, but the GWR was not really competitive as the MR had a shorter mileage, easier gradients and fewer speed restrictions, while the GWR had no less than seven restrictions of 40mph or less. Between Yate and Standish they ran over the Midland line, that company limiting the GWR to 'County' class 4-4-0s or 'La France' Atlantics, but in 1927 the restriction over Stonehouse Viaduct was relaxed to allow 'Saints' to travel over it at 30mph. In August 1900 in 24 hours Temple Meads passenger station dealt with 133 up GWR, 23 up MR, 137 down GWR, 28 down MR trains, these figures including early morning fish trains.

The Bristol to Gloucester service started with six trains each way, the fastest taking 65min. With the narrowing of the gauge in 1854 four through trains were run to Birmingham. On 6 August 1855 the MR ran excursion trains from Bristol taking 7,000 passengers to Birmingham at a return fare of 1s 6d (7½p) for 177 miles. Following the opening of the Severn Tunnel in October 1888 the GWR threatened the MR's Scottish traffic from Bristol by putting on a train which left Bristol at 9.30am and connected with a West Coast express at Crewe. The MR made a countering move by initiating a 9.35am Bristol-Leeds to connect with the Glasgow train at Normanton and the Edinburgh express at Leeds. It craftily avoided Birmingham so that passengers were not tempted to travel via the LNWR. Another disadvantage to the MR was that the GWR controlled bookings west of Bristol and therefore routed passengers through the Severn Tunnel. 1897 saw the introduction of dining cars between Bristol and Bradford, while two years later a completely new and lavishly equipped train was put on to woo passengers. By 1914 the best Derby-Bristol time had been reduced to 2hr 57min – 13min better than in 1900. Expresses stopped at Gloucester and Cheltenham but in 1908 a non-stop was introduced between Bristol and Birmingham. From 17 July 1933 Compound 4-4-0s had to achieve a mile a minute average on the 10.25am and 2.25pm from Bristol, taking the eight coaches over the 31.9 miles from Mangotsfield to Gloucester in 31 minutes. On the first day of this working, Driver J.D. James of Bristol took No 1025 with 246 tons on the 10.25 to Gloucester in 31min 8sec and the afternoon train was hauled by Class 2 No 513. The prewar up 'Devonian' was the fastest. It left Temple Meads at 12.35pm and, stopping at Gloucester and Cheltenham, reached New Street at 2.31pm. In the summer of 1956 it left Bristol at 12.30pm and arrived New Street 2.58pm, though the distance was a little longer as that year it had been re-routed via Filton instead of Mangotsfield. The 'Devonian', named in 1927, was a misnomer for half the year because only three coaches ran from Bradford to Paignton, the rest terminating at Bristol. About 1937 the introduction of 'Jubilees' allowed 83min to be saved between Leeds and Bristol and 53min Nottingham-Bristol. From the summer of 1952 the 'Cornishman' ran from Wolverhampton and Birmingham to Penzance.

In the days of the New Passage to Portskewett ferry, the service from Bristol to South Wales was unreliable depending on weather and tides, steamers sometimes being unable to leave the piers and sometimes not able to land. When Portskewett Pier was destroyed by fire 23 May 1881, passengers were carried throughout by rail to South Wales via the MR, across the Severn Bridge to Lydney and the South Wales line. This route took 2¼hr, or 25min less than the more direct ferry, but only lasted until 15 June when temporary repairs made the pier available once more. The Severn Tunnel was used for local traffic from 1 December 1886 saving 75min on the journey from Bristol to Cardiff. It was first used by London to South Wales passenger trains on 1 July 1887, trains travelling via Bristol and adding to the congestion

Right: No D164 (later No 46.027) emerging from Fishponds Tunnel with the 10.40am to Newcastle, 19 April 1969. *H. Ballantyne*

Centre right: 'Western' class No D1030 *Western Musketeer* at Narroways Hill Junction with the 08.10 Penzance-Liverpool on 6 May 1969. *H. Ballantyne*

Bottom right: Three-car dmu passing Mangotsfield North Junction with 11.25 Bristol-Worcester, 19 April 1969. *H. Ballantyne*

there as the Badminton cut-off had yet to be built. To avoid turning the engine at Temple Meads, Cardiff-Portsmouth trains made Stapleton Road their main Bristol station, though today these trains reverse at Temple Meads. Motive power has shown a considerable variety, 'Hymeks' beginning in the summer of 1961, four years later changing to Inter-City dmus to simplify reversal at Temple Meads. The introduction of a regular two hourly interval service Bristol-Portsmouth saw the appearance of SR 3H units and as a result of the growth of patronage a revised service from 1 July 1974 used either 3H or cross-country units in six-car formation. During late September 1976 many Eastleigh-based 3H demus were out of service and Class 33 locomotives hauled rakes of 4-TC units on 3H diagrams. A revised service in May 1977 saw Portsmouth trains hauled by Class 31s which in May 1980 were replaced by '33's.

Because of gradients of 1 in 60, the four daily trains from Bristol to Radstock took an hour for the 16 miles. In 1913, nine down passenger trains ran daily over the BNSR from Bristol, two of these originating from Portishead, one from Weston super Mare and another from Wells. Of the eight up, two came from Wells and Portishead. Following nationalisation the service was well-maintained while the 5.55pm fast, carrying express headlights and calling only at Radstock and Pensford, connected with the up Channel Islands boat train. With a decline in the number of passengers, the service over the branch was halved in September 1958 and totally withdrawn just over a year later. In the 1930s the line was used by Saturdays only summer expresses from Birmingham to Weymouth.

The Portishead branch had an initial service of six trains each way soon increased to eight. On 8 July 1929 a half-hourly service was introduced, one train starting from Temple Meads and the other from Ashton Gate, trains crossing at Pill or Portbury Shipyard. Because of this more intensive service, only having one platform at Portishead led to operating problems, so the carriage loop was converted into a passenger loop to serve a second platform which came into use on 9 March 1930. The line closed to passengers on 7 September 1964.

On the Henbury line a steam railmotor ran seven trips each way except on Sundays, but Temple Meads was so crowded that only two down and three up Henbury trains could use it, the others terminating at Stapleton Road. The Henbury line was also used by through passenger

Left: '481' class 2-4-0 with up train at Clifton Bridge in the 1890s. *Bristol Museum*

Below left: No 5512 with down Portishead train, Pylle Hill, c1936. *NRM*

Below: No 41203 with 8.21am Witham-Yatton-Bristol arriving at Temple Meads on 9 May 1959. *M. Mensing*

trains between London and Avonmouth connecting with Canadian and Jamaican boats. The line was closed to passenger traffic on 23 November 1964.

Initially the Bristol Port Railway & Pier ran six trains each way daily and five up and four down on Sundays. The incumbent of Shirehampton and some parishioners asked that no trains be run on a Sunday, so Sabbath trains ran through Shirehampton without stopping. This caused inconvenience to firms who were obliged to send on Sundays their shipping clerks and pilots to Pill and across the ferry to Shirehampton. Passenger services from Bristol to Clifton Down began on 1 October 1874 with 13 MR (from Mangotsfield) and 10 GWR (from Temple Meads) trains daily, with seven GWR trains on Sundays, but no Midland service. In February 1876 a through service was started between Clifton Down and Weston super Mare. When Clifton Down trains began running through to Avonmouth the GWR continued to run from Temple Meads, but the Midland started from St Philip's and ran via Clifton Junction and Easton Road Junction to the BSWUR, these two junctions being laid specially for the service. After nearly a month, it ceased, but the service from Mangotsfield and Fishponds continued until March 1941, with a break from January 1917 to May 1919. In August 1887 six trains ran each way between Temple Meads and Avonmouth, plus 26 down and 24 up to Clifton Down and 11 down and 12 up Fishponds to Clifton Down. Prior to World War 1 a through train ran from Bath (Queen Square) to Clifton Down composed of Somerset & Dorset Railway coaches and hauled by a Midland engine. With the closure of the Hotwells line in 1922, six down and four additional up

trains were provided between Clifton Down and Avonmouth Dock. 23 June 1928 many of the Avonmouth trains were extended to Severn Beach, a developing riverside resort. By 1947 the service to Avonmouth had increased to 33 each way and 18 on Sundays. Regular interval services began 3 January 1955 with two single ex-GWR single diesel railcars and a 3-car unit rostered with steam. Trains left Temple Meads every hour, with some in between at peak periods. On weekdays through services were run to Portishead and to Keynsham and Somerdale. Due to the June 1961 fare increase having lost the railway a considerable amount of traffic, a reduced timetable was inaugurated 5 March 1962. The poorer service lost more traffic and the schoolchildren's train was withdrawn. This was unfortunate as the railway's chief asset, Clifton Down Tunnel, enabled trains to beat the bus journey between the city centre and north-west Bristol by 15 to 20min. About 1911 through fast excursion trains were run from Clifton Down to London, these frequently departing at 4am and arriving back 24hr later. A special football service was run from Clifton Down to Ashton Gate near Bristol City Football Ground, while on Bank Holidays normal service was suspended and through trains run to Weston super Mare. On these days all engines carried a disc on the buffer beam, a cross denoting a special, while ordinary trains bore an oval. In 1938 the LMS attempted to popularise Severn Beach and ran through excursions via Clifton Down from Redditch, Great Malvern, Birmingham and Gloucester. Excursions to Clifton Down for Bristol Zoo, known as 'monkey specials', have always been popular, a total of 340,000 passengers was dealt

with at this station from 1958-66, though the closure of the Welsh Valleys lines, coupled with the opening of the Severn Bridge in 1966, caused the traffic to decline by 54%. Since 1971 'monkey specials' from South Wales have used the new chord line between Patchway Junction and Filton West Junction, obviating the need for a locomotive to run round the train at Stoke Gifford or Stapleton Road. This chord line was constructed from material recovered from Ashley Hill Junction to Narroways Hill Junction when that line was singled.

The first sorting coaches, four in number, were ordered by the GPO in July 1841 for use between London and Bristol and four second class coaches were adapted for carrying day mail bags and a guard; then on 1 February 1855 the world's first special postal train was inaugurated between London and Bristol. Leaving Paddington at 8.46pm it arrived Temple Meads at 12.30am, its up counterpart leaving Bristol at 12.35am and arriving at 4.10. It was usually a very light train of two sorting coaches and a van. Officially called the 'Special Mail', to the staff it was the 'Little Mail'. The vans were worked beyond Bristol to and from Plymouth by ordinary passenger trains. From June 1869 it ceased to be solely for postal traffic and one first class coach was attached; accommodation was so limited that even directors who wished to travel by this train had to apply for a special pass. A Plymouth to Bristol TPO commenced 1 December 1859 and connected with the North Mail, on

11 February 1896 becoming the Bristol & Penzance TPO (North Mail), the Bristol & Plymouth TPO on 14 April 1930 and ceased running on 3 March 1972. In the days of Ocean Mails from Plymouth a van was slipped at Bedminister for Bristol. In March 1855 the Bristol-Newcastle mail was inaugurated, the van being the only item of coaching stock to carry the letters M&NEJS. By 1885 it used the TPO apparatus at Fishponds. The TPOs were suspended during World War 2. Today there is a 19.34 TPO to Newcastle, the 17.35 from Leeds has a TPO from Derby and returns at 01.10. The up and down 'Postal', the 22.25 Paddington-Penzance and the 19.35 Penzance-Paddington are both at Temple Meads at the same time and the GPO sorting staff change over. The 01.24 to Milford Haven conveys a TPO to Carmarthen. BR staff handle GPO parcel post in wooden MATES, but GPO staff handle letters in mailbags. The quantity of mail dealt with at Temple Meads not infrequently exceeds station time as patterns of traffic change and cannot always be timetabled.

An all year round Motorail service runs from Bristol as tail traffic on the 16.08 to Newcastle, while during he summer a thrice weekly service runs to Stirling and a weekly service to Edinburgh. An ancestor of today's Raildrive car hire service in the 1840s saw post horses kept ready at Temple Meads to draw carriages from the Clifton district to Temple Meads.

On summer Saturdays some up holiday trains used the

avoiding line to ease congestion at Temple Meads, but had to foul the down line to reach it, then had to wait their turn to get on the Bath to Bristol line at North Somerset Junction and blocked the up line to attain the South Wales line at Dr Day's Bridge Junction where they fouled the down South Wales line. Trains using this route tended to lose time and the only solution to the difficulty would have been to have built flyovers which would have been quite uneconomic as they were only really required for a maximum of 15 days a year. One interesting train using the avoiding line in 1952 was the 9.52am (SO) from Weston super Mare to New Street, usually worked throughout by a Midland engine which did not regain its own metals until Yate.

When the Bristol to London line was being discussed at a GWR Board meeting, a director expressed concern at the length of the line and Brunel replied, 'Why not make it longer and have a steamboat go from Bristol to New York and call it the "Great Western"?' He may have said it partly in fun, but Thomas Guppy seized the idea and the Great Western Steamship Company was formed, the *Great Western* sailing from Bristol 8 April 1838 and reaching New York in 15 days 10hr. Although passenger

sailings from Bristol did not develop on a large scale, there were some from Avonmouth. Quite early in the town's history, a passenger platform and waiting room were provided at the landward end of the East Pier and later a timber passenger station was built at the South Pier, the GWR manning the booking office. Boat trains in connection with the West Indies service ran fortnightly, Port of Bristol Authority's locomotives working GWR coaches over the dock lines, but latterly traffic did not warrant a whole train and just two or three coaches were attached to a Paddington to Bristol express and worked specially to Avonmouth. The passenger station was destroyed in World War 2 and a platform at the South Transit Shed was used. The last boat train was worked on 26 August 1964. In addition to passengers to the West Indies, immigrant ships left Avonmouth and trains carrying them to the docks were required to be locked when passengers had alighted and not used again until after being disinfected. Sometimes Campbell's White Funnel line ran paddle boat excursions from the docks, passengers arriving by special train.

Number of trains daily from Bristol, including Stapleton Road is shown in the table below.

To	Sept 1850	July 1913	July 1939	May 1980
London	9	15	12+1SX	26
Plymouth	No through trains	9	12+1MX +7SO	15+5SO +1MO
Portsmouth	on these lines	4 from TM	1 from TM 3 from S Rd. +2SO S Rd.	7+2SO
Cardiff		10 from TM 3 from S Rd	17+1SX TM 7+1SX TM 7+1FX S Rd	17+4SO
Birmingham	5	16	3+2SO 1 from S Rd.	15+1MX 7SO 1FO

Above left: **Boat train at Port of Bristol's 'New Station' at Avonmouth in the early 1920s.** *Port of Bristol Authority*

Above: **PBA loco at Avonmouth drawing train of passengers to Royal Edward Dock for the first postwar Campbell's paddle steamer trip.** *M. Farr*

Right: **Yellow cross dividing Platforms 4 & 3, 29 May 1980.** Author

Temple Meads, the principal Bristol station, in 1935 was used by over 400 passenger trains daily, it being the most important exchange station on the GWR – routes converging from London, Exeter, Southampton, Bournemouth, Weymouth, South Wales and the Midlands. Over five million passengers used it that year, a further three and a half million using the suburban stations of Stapleton Road, Lawrence Hill and Bedminster, while 10 million passengers passed through on their journey. Following the closure of the Brunel train shed the platforms were renumbered starting from the north and working south, instead of the reverse as had been the case with the 1935 renumbering. Today No 1 is the east end bay, just long enough for a locomotive and three coaches and used for Severn Beach and some Cardiff trains; No 2 is a parcels bay at the west end of the station while the other ten are long through platforms subdivided into two, the actual division being marked by a suspended rectangular plate carrying a yellow 'X' on a black ground, the odd numbered platforms being at the east and the even numbers at the west end. No 13 is now exclusively for parcels traffic. One of five assistant station managers is in charge of the overall working and under him is a station supervisor overseeing the platform staff, while each platform is in the care of a chargeman. Because the curved platforms hamper visibility, there is a special departure procedure. Not more than two minutes before the booked departure time the platform chargeman presses a 'Train Ready to Start' button which signals to the panel box. The announcer asks passengers to close the doors and stand clear. An RA (Right away) sign lights up beside the starting signal and the driver opens up. As a safety precaution platform staff must not give 'right away' to the guard unless the starting signal is off and as this cannot be seen due to the curve, a white light for the staff in the centre of the platform reads 'OFF' when the signal is green.

Today supervisory staff are all in radio contact which saves the time and trouble of finding a phone and is particularly valuable in busy periods. About 150 passenger trains depart from Temple Meads every 24hr increasing to approximately 190 on a summer Saturday. A particularly wide variety of trains can be seen – main line, cross-country, dmu, loco-hauled vacuum-braked coaches, locomotive-hauled air-braked coaches, HSTs, Motorail and sleeping car trains. It is an Inter-City station with little commuter traffic as the station is too far from shops and offices and the city is well-served by road. Bristol has advertised that it is at the centre of motorways

and railways and, since the introduction of HSTs, business houses have moved from London to Bristol; the Avon Country Structure Plan proposes 535,000 sq m of extra office space, nearly half of this in central Bristol. Most local traffic comes from the Severn Beach line and in 1978 1,500 passenger trips were made on a winter weekday, 1,900 during school summer holidays and 1,000 on Saturdays both summer and winter. Only 3% of passengers on the line travel outside Avon and only 4% travel to stations within Avon and off the branch. The nine peak hour journeys account for 66% of the passengers. Deficit on the line is met by a Public Service Obligation Grant and the line provides the only public transport between Severn Beach and Avonmouth. A special wheelchair and lift service is provided at Temple Meads for invalids, an average of about 40 disabled people a week are dealt with throughout the year. Being a large station it suffers a fair number of mishaps to passengers, (through no negligence of the railway), people tumbling or feeling unwell. While the author was speaking to an assistant station manager, a message came through that a passenger had gashed himself, but insisted on catching his train. The railway rang his destination station asking them to check that he was all right on his arrival.

The Travel Centre at Temple Meads is the largest in the West of England. It differs from its predecessor – the booking office – in that it is outward rather than inward looking – the aim of the centre being to actively sell BR, not just wait for customers to come. BR products are sold vigorously. When HSTs were introduced on the London line, the centre sold a limited number of special tickets to London 'Go at 125mph for 125 pence' while another venture was the record-breaking Jubilee run. Airline tickets are supplied by the centre within 24hr. One achievement of the centre is that out of 6,000 Bristol University students, 4,000 hold student railcards. The centre opened in 1973 has a carpeted lounge, and nameplates change salespeople into persons. Apart from continental inquiries, the staff do everything – sell tickets, make reservations and answer timetable queries. Travel centre, as distinct from ticket window, sales run at £1million a year. Thirty staff are employed plus the manager. In 1980 £5million in passenger fares was taken at the station representing about 700,000 tickets, a booking clerk taking £2,000 to £3,000 on each turn of duty. Of the six immediate ticket selling positions, the three centre ones receive the most use, so to give the National Cash Register ticket machines equal use, they are changed periodically to different windows. Ultimatic issuing machines and tickets (pre-printed rolls) are used for issuing popular tickets as they can be dispensed faster than NCR tickets, while a Flexiprinter is used for printing tickets for bulk supply to firms. Flexiprinters are only found at large stations such as Temple Meads, as the blocks required for printing are expensive. 1,500 phone inquiries are received daily and staff deal with up to eight lines. BR Awaydays are competitive with buses, tending to be cheaper and noticeably so in the case of travel to or from Bristol suburban stations as there is a flat rate to

Left: Light indicating to platform staff that starting signal is off, 29 May 1980. *Author*

Top: Class 08 No 08.951 at Temple Meads drawing sleeping cars from 23.45 ex-Edinburgh on 5 July 1975. *Author*

Above: Dmu No W55001, leaving the main line with the 13.05 Temple Meads-Severn Beach service. At Narroways Hill Junction north of Stapleton Road, 6 May 1969. *H. Ballantyne*

Right: Booking office windows, Temple Meads, 30 May 1980. *Author*

Bristol making travel from Temple Meads to a suburban station 'free'.

In the early 1900s a wide variety of coaches belonging to various companies could be seen at Temple Meads. Apart from GWR and MR coaches there were through Somerset & Dorset coaches to Bournemouth, Great Central coaches on through trains from Ilfracombe to Halifax and Leeds, and Taunton to Leicester; London & North Western coaches from Plymouth to Manchester; a West Coast Joint Stock coach ran from Exeter to Glasgow while Caledonian coaches ran Bristol to Edinburgh. The only carriage sidings now at Bristol are at Malago Vale west of Bedminster and have a capacity of 133. In June 1980 five sets of Mk I coaches were kept for north-east/south-west services; eight Portsmouth/ Weymouth sets and one maintenance spare. At Malago Vale some sets are just a 'run round' and given a simple brushing out, while those standing all day are cleaned more thoroughly, minor repairs such as broken steps and worn brake blocks being dealt with. Sleeping car berths are made up and the newspaper and TPO trains cleaned and stabled. A shore plug is provided for electric heating, while steam heating comes from either a boiler house containing a 'Western' class boiler, or a portable boiler. A mechanical coach washing plant was opened at Pylle Hill 19 September 1967 where coaches have a pre-wet, acidic solution applied, then akaline solution and rinse. The brushes are turned electrically. Trains are supposed to pass through at 2mph and if they pass through too fast, the apparatus is automatically turned off. More recently an HST experimental nose end washing plant has been added. Other carriage sidings have now been closed. Dr Day's Bridge Carriage Sidings were situated north-west of Temple Meads either side of the South Wales line and were built under a 1930 Government loan as was Malago Vale. Marsh Pond Sidings east of St Philip's Marsh opened in 1917 was used for non-corridor and excursion stock. Other sidings were at Ashton Gate and Filton West Junction, while Bristol West Sidings were four short looped lines at Pylle Hill. The MR carriage shed was at Barrow Road.

As Bristol is an important junction, signalling is vital. In 1909 Temple Meads was controlled by four boxes, two of which contained 105 levers each. With the extension of the station in 1935 the signalling was renewed. Bristol Temple Meads East power box was the largest on the GWR and replaced two mechanical boxes, Temple Meads East and South Wales Junction. It had 23 block bells, each having a different tone and was in communication with no less than seven adjacent boxes. Its architecture was 'avant garde' and still looked modern when replaced 35 years later. It had three storeys, whereas the similar West and Loco boxes had but two. The exteriors were of red brick in Flemish bond relieved by white stone lintels and sills. Points were operated by Metro Vickers GRS model 5A dc machines fed from a 120V battery situated in the cabin. The East box had 368 'levers' which were actually slides pulled to halfway

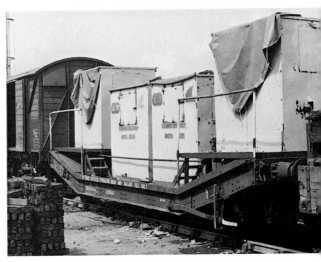

Left: Malago Vale Carriage Sidings. Newspaper train in centre, 30 May 1980. *Author*

Above: Muck wagon for coach rubbish. Malago Vale Sidings, 30 May 1980. *Author*

Below: Type 4 No D1952 passes Malago Vale Sidings hauling the 08.45 Wolverhampton-Taunton train on Saturday 17 August 1968. *P.J. Fowler*

Below: Electric heating switches, Malago Vale Sidings, 30 May 1980.   *Author*

Bottom: Portable generator for charging coach batteries, Malago Vale Siding, 30 May 1980.   *Author*

Right: No D1648 heads into Bristol with stock from Malago Vale for the 13.15 to Paddington on 9 March 1968. *D. Wharton*

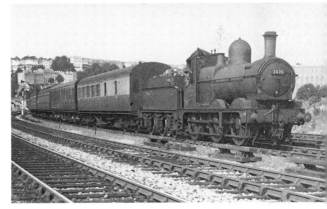

Top: Prototype HST nose end cleaner (lt) and washer, Pylle Hill, 31 July 1980. *Author*

Above: Ashton Gate Carriage Sidings. *M.E.J. Deane*

Left: No 46.006 at Pylle Hill with coaches from Malago Vale for the 13.48 Temple Meads-Birmingham. *Author*

Top: Signals in cutting which was formerly Bristol No 1 Tunnel opened out 1897-9. *GWR*

Above: Bristol Temple Meads East box, 26 March 1935. *GWR*

Top right: Bristol Temple Meads East box, 22 November 1960. *BR*

Right: Colour light signal newly installed for MAS scheme, temporarily covered over until it is brought into use. In the background are some of the colour light signals dating from 1933-4. *BR*

Above: One of the first installations of the new Atlas 'Haline' floodlighting helping round-the-clock completion of the MAS scheme. *BR*

Right: One of the few mechanical boxes still in the Bristol area. Driver of dmu Temple Meads to Severn Beach collects the single line tablet at Hallen Marsh signalbox, 25 July 1974. *Author*

position where they locked until the point or colour light signal had functioned correctly when they could then be pulled out to their fullest extent. Three special class signalmen were always on duty plus a booking boy. Bristol West had 328 levers and 20 bells and was also manned by three men and a boy.

With a view to economies through closing 70 signalboxes and saving 343 staff, in 1970 Multiple Aspect Signalling operated from one box at Bristol was installed at a cost of about £4million and controlled 114 route miles from Cogload Junction to Bradford Junction, Corsham, Badminton, Charfield, Pilning and Avonmouth. The resignalling would have been hard to justify financially without track rationalisation, especially that at Temple Meads which has allowed trains to be handled more expeditiously at fewer platforms, the simplified layout also permitting the speed limit approaching the station to be raised from 10 to 25mph. Through programming of locomotives largely obviated engine changes at Temple Meads reducing the number of

within three or four miles of Bristol are operated by individual circuits over a telephone type non-vital cable; beyond this distance, electronic time division multiplex equipment is used. Current supplies are obtained from the electricity board at various sites and transformed to 650V single-phase ac for distribution along the track. Lineside hot box detectors are installed on both lines at Coalpit Heath and at Nailsea on the up. They alert signalmen at Bristol of up to four hot boxes on one train, together with their positions in the train. Normal staff on a shift is three signalmen at the main panel, one at the subsidiary panel, two standby men, a train recorder, a train announcer, a panel supervisor and a communications supervisor. BR's own telephone exchange is in the same building and at times of maximum telephone traffic, four operators deal with 900 extensions.

And what of passenger traffic of the future? An Avon Metro has been proposed based on Bristol and using existing, or abandoned railways outside the city centre and a new underground section in the heart of the city. This scheme would enable passengers to make fuller use of the area's railways, as, because of the poor siting of Temple Meads, only about 1,200 workers use the railway daily and since the closure of most of Bristol's suburban lines, there is not a rail based public transport system sufficiently attractive to offer a realistic alternative to car.

The five Metro routes suggested are:

1 Metropolitan line: Portishead to Yate, utilising existing goods line and the bed of the former MR line Fishponds – Mangotsfield.
2 Brunel line: Bath Spa to Avonmouth loop via Shirehampton or Filton.
3 Imperial line: Weston super Mare to Brislington and diverging to Bishopsworth and Whitchurch.
4 Plimsol line: Severn Beach to Bristol.
5 Concorde line: Weston super Mare to Bath via Fishponds, Warmley and joining the former GWR line west of Bath. Car parks would be provided at selected stations.

movements required, the average time a train spent at a platform being reduced from 18 minutes in 1938 to 4 minutes in 1976. Statistics of Bristol Panel Box when opened:

No of point machines	243
No of controlled signals (2, 3 & 4 aspect	163
No of automatic signals (2, 3 & 4 aspect)	117
No of track circuits (functional)	556
No of ground frames	50
No of level crossings	3
No of WR AWS ramps	200
No of BR AWS indicators	24
No of telephones – signal posts	268
– ground frames etc	124

The box has two separate consoles: the main covering Cogload Junction-Temple Meads-Corsham, also Bradford Junction and the four track section to Stapleton Road; while the subsidiary console deals with Stapleton Road-Pilning, Badminton and Charfield. Three aspect multi-lens signals are used, but four-aspect signalling has been installed on certain sections where an improved headway is required, for example between Westerleigh and Stoke Gifford where the two tracks carry the former Midland service in addition to other traffic, and also through the Temple Meads station area where closer spacing is required for crossing movements. Interlockings

Initial capital expenditure at 1979 prices for the construction of new track, adaptation of existing track formations, station building and refurbishing is £117million, while rolling stock of the Tyne & Wear type would cost £44million and a further £55million would be required to complete the scheme. Bill Kent when BR West of England Divisional Manager said he was confident that with careful timetabling Avon Metro trains could share existing BR lines with HSTs.

An Avon Metro would more than halve travelling times: 11 minutes by Metro from Whitchurch to the city centre compared with 30 minutes by bus, but in view of the curtailment of public spending, the plan, though admirable overall for time and fuel economy, may not be made a reality and in its Structure Plan, Avon County Council stresses the high priority of an adequate road network for industry and commerce.

Above: MAS box at Temple Meads.   *BR*   *Below:* Engineers testing equipment in the MAS box.   *BR*

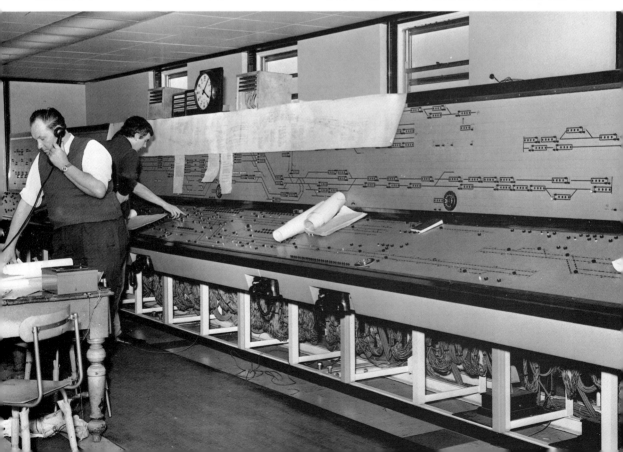

Development of Freight Services

Bristol was the focal point of three broad gauge companies, the GWR, B&E and Bristol & Gloucester, but development of freight traffic was hampered by the fact that until the 1860s and 70s there was no rail access to the docks. Lines to Avonmouth and Portishead were opened in 1865 and 1867, but at first handled passengers rather than freight. The city docks received a partial rail access when the Bristol Harbour line was opened in 1872, but wharves at Canon's Marsh were left unserved and city merchants proposed various schemes to link them with the main lines. As many ships were too large to navigate the river to Bristol, Avonmouth grew in importance. In 1900 it was selected as the port for the fortnightly Imperial West Indies mail service, while in March 1901 the first consignment of bananas arrived, Elders & Fyffes inaugurating a fortnightly service from Port Limon, Costa Rica. Until 1967 when the traffic ceased, bananas were important. In the winter months 600 GWR banana vans had to be preheated to 68°F and 10 fitted brake vans lettered 'Avonmouth RU' were allocated to the traffic. The LMS also ran banana trains, one leaving Avonmouth at 3.50pm and arriving at St Pancras at 3.8am. Traffic in the years following World War 2 was heavy and when two banana boats arrived within a week, 700 vans needed to be strawed in the week before their arrival, tared (weighed empty), loaded and then grossed (weighed full). Wagons of loose straw, known as 'wagons of wind', came mainly from stations on the Badminton line. Petroleum was another important commodity and as early as 1911, 27 oil tanks were set in the vicinity of the docks and in 1919 an oil basin was

Below: **The Mayoress of Bristol cutting the first sod of the Harbour Tramway, 8 October 1863.** *Author's collection*

Left: Loading GWR bulk grain wagons, Avonmouth, October 1936.   *Port of Bristol Authority*

Centre left: SS *Ariguani* discharging bananas at Avonmouth, 24 June 1947. *Port of Bristol Authority*

Bottom left: PBA loco and timber train of internal use wagons at Avonmouth. *Port of Bristol Authority*

Top right: South African coal being discharged into rail wagons, Avonmouth, 11 April 1980.   *Author*

Right: Tractor shunting coal wagons at Avonmouth Docks, 11 April 1980. *Author*

added to the Royal Edward Docks. Today no oil goes by rail. The 1½ million tons hauled over the Port of Bristol Authority's lines in 96,506 wagons by 21 PBA diesel and seven steam locomotives in 1964 has decreased considerably; cattle food for instance, which used to go by rail to small country stations most of which were closed in the Beeching era, now goes by road. Several large firms at Avonmouth still use rail transport, regular traffic being chemicals, fertilisers, zinc, lead, tin concentrates, copper and coal, while other commodities to and from the docks are variable. BR benefits because the dock dues are less than many other ports which makes it cheaper to unload at Avonmouth and then send goods on to their destination by rail. It is interesting that

some firms in the area which abandoned rail for road transport, quickly came back to it again, finding the alternative giving a far poorer service.

Avonmouth was very important during both world wars. In addition to its normal trains, extra traffic had to be catered for; for example, horses and mules destined for the army, 89 truck loads being despatched on one day alone and 65,956 mules arriving in less than eight months. An example of the troop traffic can be seen in the figures for 7-11 February 1915, when 92 trains consisting of 2,093 loaded coaches, vans, horse boxes, cattle vans and open trucks were hauled by PBA locomotives from the Exchange Sidings to the embarkation berth. During World War 2 Avonmouth

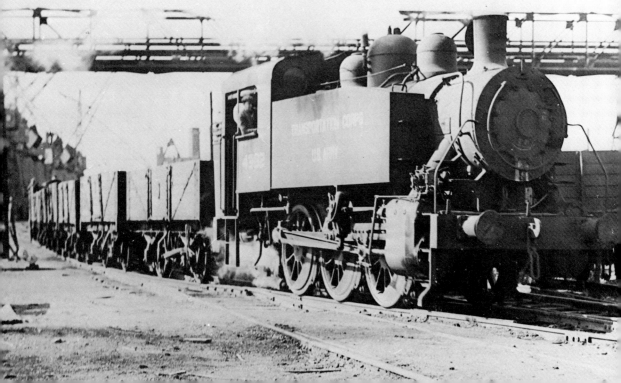

Top left: On 3 March 1944 Red Cross train leaves Avonmouth Docks after loading patients from hospital ship *Somersetshire*.   *Port of Bristol Authority*

Left: USA-built 0-6-0T on loan to PBA at work on 30 August 1944.   *Port of Bristol Authority.*

Top: Nos 1990 and 1999 USA 0-6-0Ts from SS *Glenifer* being placed in barges to speed unloading at the Royal Edward Dock, Avonmouth, 24 March 1944.   *Port of Bristol Authority*

Above: PBA wagons at Avonmouth. Left hand wagon has spot showing it can run over BR metals, 11 April 1980. *Author*

Left: 0-6-OPT on up goods, Clifton Bridge. *M.E.J. Deane*

Below left: Sally, GWR horse No 503, with parcels van by former B&E offices, 1942. *R. Thomas*

Below: 'Aberdare' class No 2630 passing Temple Meads with transfer freight 1934. *NRM*

again became of vital importance to the country as it was one of the ports to receive supplies from America. Today, the PBA's fleet of 2,150 open wagons and vans at Avonmouth and 80 at Portishead has been reduced to about 500 at Avonmouth alone. PBA lines still connect with its trading estate at Chittening providing direct connection from ship to factory, a red spot on some wagons indicating that they can run over BR lines.

Goods traffic on the Portishead line was less important than that from Avonmouth, timber, grain, beans and petroleum being the main items. Phosphorous was manufactured at Portishead and the finished product distributed in specially built rail tank wagons. A woodpulp terminal opened at Portishead dock in the early 1970s and until December 1976, pulp was loaded into a bulk train for the journey to Marsh Pond, Bristol. The BNSR served the Radstock coalfield and in 1913 eight down goods and mineral trains ran over the line compared with nine passenger trains. With the closure of the Somerset & Dorset line on 6 March 1966 all coal traffic from Radstock was carried over the former BNSR line, but an unusually violent rainstorm on 10 July 1968 washed away part of the embankment north of Pensford station and as it was uneconomic to repair this slip, coal traffic to Portishead power station and Imperial Smelting Processes Ltd, Avonmouth, was diverted via Frome.

The five outwards platforms in the 1876 Temple Meads goods depot were divided into 16 loading berths

according to districts and trains, a unique practice being that all carmen employed either by the GWR or by private firms, when bringing in goods were required to deliver them to a particular berth, thus reducing porterage and trucking to a minimum. The carmen usually loaded the lorries in the city in such a manner as to facilitate unloading at the different berths. It was rare for goods to be dropped off at the wrong berth because each checker had a good knowledge of the stations served by his berth. At platforms where there were two loading lines, access to the wagons on the second line was by placing a loading board across from the inner to the outer wagon. In 1914 competition for parcels traffic at Bristol was so great that the GWR paid a tonnage bonus to parcel van men and they tried hard to get traffic which was consigned to the MR route. In the 1920s, between three and five pm, approximately 200 loads (2,000 consignments) were carted into the depot. Wagons arriving were placed on the line serving the long No 1 platform and after being unloaded were worked by gravitation and capstan shunters to the bottleneck road at the Victoria Street end of the yard, from where they were worked by capstans into the long storage siding, or into the outward loading lines. As outwards traffic from the depot was about 50% greater than inwards, these wagons were insufficient to supply the requirements of the outwards side, but the arrangement reduced very considerably the number of empty wagons which had to

Above left: No 5626 with down freight, 2 May 1953. *R.E. Toop*

Left: D1056 *Western Sultan* in maroon livery at Narroways Hill Junction with 11.40 coal empties Lawrence Hill-Radyr, 8 May 1969. *H. Ballantyne*

Above: No D7012 with goods train north of Stapleton Road passes between buttresses of line which ran from Ashley Hill Junction–Kingswood Junction, 6 May 1969. *H. Ballantyne*

Right: No 7032 and No 1942 at Temple Meads. *G.R. Hounsell*

Below right: No 6811 *Cranbourne Grange* with down parcels train leaving Temple Meads on 25 April 1953. *R.E. Toop*

be brought into the shed by locomotives and placed into position for unloading.

Traffic from east of Bristol was made up into through trucks for principal West of England stations to the extent of 30 wagons a day, while traffic in the reverse direction was made up at Canon's Marsh and despatched in about 45 trucks. When there was insufficient traffic at Temple Meads to make a through or transfer wagon for the West of England, the goods were carted to Canon's Marsh for loading in through wagons from that depot, a similar arrangement applying in the reverse direction.

Today most parcels are dealt with at Temple Meads passenger station on Platforms Nos 2 and 13, one gang working on each platform but deployed as required since parcel trains may be worked into other platforms. Most parcels trains arrive during the night and come from Peterborough, Nottingham, Crewe, Bradford, Eastleigh and Newport, the majority of trains having regular vans for Bristol. The portering staff offload the BRUTES (BR Universal Trolley Equipment) by fork lift truck, place them in a lift and draw them into a subway below the station. A cob (electric battery tractor) takes them to the parcels depot for premium sorting where parcels are placed into bays for various roads in towns or villages and rounds are made to the area enclosed by Warminister, Weston super Mare, Wells, Street and Thornbury. A maximum of about 4,500 parcels a day are handled. Carmen and vans in BR livery are hired from National Carriers Ltd, drivers collecting about 3,000 parcels during the day and bringing them in during the afternoon. On arrival they are coded for their destination, placed in BRUTES and sent up to the appropriate platform. A BRUTE repair shop is situated below the station and trolleys come for repair from all over the country. Temple Meads is one of the main transfer points between the

various Red Star services, Red Star being a parcel delivered by nominated passenger and parcels trains. Bristol is the terminus of a newspaper train. Packers from wholesale newsagents travel up by HST, returning in the newspaper train making packets for newsagents. The train consists of adapted GUVs equipped with tables, a toilet and corridor connections.

Goods trains came to Bristol from many parts of the country. The 1.30am Old Oak Common to Stoke Gifford was known as 'Long Tom' because it often consisted of 100 wagons, while the 5.10am Avonmouth to Weymouth was one of five animal feeding stuff trains which left Avonmouth between midnight and 6am. The 2.25pm Paddington to Temple Meads, known as the 'Paddy Mail' called at all stations and arrived at 10pm with a load of anything from two to 22 vans and hauled by any tender engine up to a 'King'. Its return working, known as the 'Cocoa', started in 1905 as the first GWR vacuum brake fitted goods trains. Circa 1914 it was often worked by 4-6-2 No 111 *The Great Bear* which hauled 70 wagons from East Depot to Acton in 3hr 5min. Later the train was usually handled by a '47xx' class 2-8-0. In the 1920s 15 trains left Temple Meads good depot between 5pm and 2.30am: seven were through trains running to such places as Birkenhead, Birmingham, Manchester, London, Carmarthen and Weymouth, while others were transfer trips connecting with through trains starting from the concentration shunting yards at East Depot, West Depot and Stoke Gifford.

Bristol is the freight centre for the area and has had a TOPS office since 1975, the Total Operational Processing System giving by computer a nationwide view of what traffic is in transit for the area as no wagon can move without being reported. TOPS enables both BR and firms to plan ahead. At the time of writing goods into

Bristol are principally steel, paper, woodpulp, china clay, chocolate, cereals, fertiliser, coke, cement, fruit and vegetables, while outwards traffic is stone aggregate, cocoa beans, copper and other metals, sea-weed (from South America to Oban for table jellies and forms a part cargo to Avonmouth) and brown sugar.

The principal freight only line was the Bristol Harbour Railway built by the GWR, B&E and Bristol Corporation. Although only threequarters of a mile in length, construction was quite difficult and expensive as a long viaduct and three bridges were needed. Making the line required the demolition of a vicarage, while cutting a 282yd long tunnel involved the removal and reburial at Brislington of many bodies, the railway, of course, paying for the new burial ground. Bathurst Basin had to be crossed by an opening bascule bridge. Designed by Charles Richardson who was to become chief engineer to the Severn Tunnel, it was powered by a horizontal steam engine, now to be seen in Bristol Industrial Museum, with two cylinders 9in by 12in and built by the Avonside Engine Company at Bristol in 1872. A friction drive was fitted so that the delicately balanced 250ton bridge could not be overdriven. Mixed gauge was laid as at the time of construction both broad and narrow gauge were in use. Although not fully completed, the line was sufficiently ready for a single line mixed gauge opening on 11 March 1872, although at that date, neither of the two owning companies yet had any narrow gauge lines in the city. Soon after opening, a half mile long extension to a larger and better sited wharf at Wapping was decided on and opened 12 June 1876. When the main GWR line was blocked between Temple Meads and Parson Street on Sundays 26 April and 15 November 1931 for the demolition of two overline bridges, on both occasions passenger trains were diverted via the Harbour line,

Ashton Swing Bridge and West Loop, such an event being almost unique. With the run-down of the city docks, the line fell into disuse and was closed 11 January 1964 and east of Wapping the track, viaduct and bridges were subsequently dismantled. Today there is usually one coal train daily to Ashton Meadows siding from where Western Fuel Company's Hudswell 0-6-0 ex-PBA No D1171 takes it to Wapping Wharf.

In order to reduce carting and barging, under the Bristol Harbour Lines Act of 1897 the GWR obtained powers to connect the Harbour Railway with the Portishead branch and build an extension to Canon's Marsh on the north side of the Floating Harbour. Canon's Marsh, although close to the city docks, had not been developed because of lack of rail communication. It also planned to use Canon's Marsh to deal with all West of England goods and so reduce congestion at Temple Meads and Pylle Hill. The most interesting feature of the branch was Ashton Swing Bridge carrying the line over the New Cut. The bridge had two decks, the upper carrying a public road and the lower a double track railway and was constructed by John Lysaght & Co Ltd for £70,389. All river traffic had to pass to the north side of the pier where the opening had a clear span of 85ft. The swing span weighed 1,000tons and was 202ft 6in in length and could turn either up or down stream. As only one vessel in either direction was allowed to pass at one time, cones were provided to control shipping movements. For vessels downstream, the north cone (point upwards) was lowered and the south cone for those upstream. The yard arm on which the cones were hoisted was fixed so that both cones showed when it was open. The bridge was worked by hydraulic power, the two three-throw reversible engines being situated in a control cabin above the roadway. Two vertical shafts

Above left: 0-6-0PT No 3650 on Bathurst bascule bridge. Broad gauge rail bearer arrowed. The water pipe to Wapping Goods Yard had to be dismantled when the bridge was moved. *Port of Bristol Authority*

Left: Ivatt Class 2s double-head RCTS special approaching Ashton Swing Bridge, 28 April 1957. *H. Ballantyne*

Above: Western Fuel Company's Hudswell 0-6-0 ex-PBA No D1171 at Wapping Wharf, 18 August 1980. *Author*

Right: 0-6-0PT No 8746 by Cumberland Siding ground frame. *R. E. Toop*

Below right: Ashton Swing Bridge, view south along deck, 21 August 1980. *Author*

Left: Dean 0-6-0 proceeding along Hotwell Road to Canon's Marsh. *M.E.J. Deane*

Below: The 12.35 Temple Meads to Bath Spa dmu passing Bristol East Depot, 23 February 1968. *P.J. Fowler*

turned the span, only one engine being required, the other acting as a standby. The bridge was interlocked with GWR signalboxes on either side. The bridge has not been swung since 1936 and was made a permanent fixture in 1953. The control cabin and road deck were subsequently removed as a new road system to cope with modern traffic has been constructed in the area.

The line to Canon's Marsh led to development in the district. The gasworks had direct rail communication, a chocolate factory was built and a lead pipe and sheet factory rebuilt and extended, while a marble and slate importer set up an establishment. Lairage, cattle pens and sidings were provided, chiefly for Irish traffic, Cork and Waterford steamers discharging within a few yards and obviating a drive of a mile or two through the city to the railway. Rail access was provided to a foreign animals wharf at Merchants Dock. In an undertaking given by the GWR in return for using land belonging to the cathedral, no locomotive movements or whistling were carried out during the hours of service on Sundays. The 22 sidings in the yard accommodated 531 wagons. In 1914 115 men were employed at the depot and about 500 wagons exchanged daily, one engine shunting for 22hr daily and another for 8hr. Transfer trips were worked to various outlying marshalling yards set up on the periphery of Bristol.

Opening the Severn Tunnel to goods traffic on 1 September 1886 had its influence on Bristol causing additional congestion in the area as the avoiding line via Badminton had yet to be built. Nine goods and mineral trains ran each way daily. To cope with the extra traffic coming through the Severn Tunnel, up and down yards at Bristol East Depot were opened in 1890 west of Bristol No 1 tunnel, the up sidings being converted into a more economical gravitational yard on 7 October 1923. As rearranged, the yard consisted of 17 sidings. The first three were reception sidings to accommodate up to 131 wagons from trains waiting to be broken up by the hump shunting engine, while the remaining 14 roads were directly connected to the hump and held a total of 468 wagons. The up yard dealt with 41 trains every 24hr, involving passing an average of 1,300 wagons daily over the hump. The hump saved the cost of about 100 engine hours weekly. Points were operated from a ground frame. So that the shunter in charge of the frame was able to communicate with the driver of the shunting engine, a Klaxon horn was installed, one blast indicating 'go ahead', two 'come back', three 'stop' and six 'Obstruction-danger'. A code of engine whistles in connection with the East Depot main line signalbox was also used. Both yards at the East Depot closed 7 August 1967, the up side now being a Catchment Area Focal Point to which runable crippled wagons are consigned and the down side the Civil Engineer's Yard.

On the other side of the city, the West Depot opened in 1906, accommodating about 400 wagons plus storage for about a further 120 at Ashton Meadows sidings. In 1903 conjointly with the opening of the Badminton line, a yard at Stoke Gifford was provided to cope mainly with Avonmouth traffic. Sidings were lengthened and an additional one laid in 1918 making a total of 14 roads in the up yard and 10 in the down. Both yards closed 4 October 1971, much of the site being used for Bristol Parkway station and its adjoining car park. The MR had a similar yard to Stoke Gifford at Westerleigh with 12 roads in each of the two yards, these being taken out of use 22 February 1965, most of the traffic being transferred to Stoke Gifford. Kingsland Road depot with 23 roads on the south side of the line just east of Temple Meads was a 'full loads' depot. In 1970 it employed 40 men including 26 NCL motor drivers, but 10 years later the number had fallen to nine including two drivers. At one time about 60 wagons of coal were unloaded daily by grab for the nearby gasworks. It also dealt with livestock except to and from the West of England which was sorted at Pylle Hill, the former B&E goods depot. Pylle Hill, now reduced in size, is used for full loads of parcels. The GWR built six

Above: Class 5 No 45301 on a special from Bristol passing Stoke Gifford yard, **10 August 1963.** *D. J. Wall*

Left: No D26 passes Stoke Gifford yard with up freight, **17 October 1964.** *E. Thomas*

Below left: Westerleigh yard, view north, **21 April 1960.** *Author*

Left: Railway wagon on fire at Pylle Hill Depot. *H.C. Leat, Bristol Photographic Society, per M.J. Tozer*

Below: No D24 passes Pylle Hill Depot with empty stock for the 15.30 to York, 24 February 1968. *P.J. Fowler*

Above left: Baguley 0-4-0 shunter at Filton Coal Concentration Yard, 21 August 1980.   *Author*

Left: Filton Coal Concentration Yard: grid for hopper wagons and tipping bars for tipping end-unloading wagons. *Author*

Above: MR covered dock at Avonside Wharf, 30 May 1922.   *NRM*

Right: MR wooden steam pinnace No 1 inspection launch at Bristol.   *P. White collection*

storage sheds there for imported foodstuffs awaiting delivery. Lawrence Hill, opened in 1895, was for general goods, coal and other minerals while Stapleton Road was for station to station traffic, coal and other minerals and is now used for cement traffic, the daily brick train having ceased in 1978. St Philip's Marsh mileage depot opened in April 1893 and closed on 3 September 1973, while in 1965 some sidings at Filton Junction were lifted and the remainder sold to a coal concentration depot. Approximately 20 wagons are dealt with daily in the summer and 50 in the winter, wagons being shunted by the Bristol Mechanised Coal Company's Baguley 0-4-0DM.

The MR's Avonside goods depot had an extensive frontage on the Floating Harbour with warehouses for the storage of flour, grain, cheese, sugar, tinned foods, dried fruit and other merchandise. The company maintained a fleet of 19 120ton barges for use to and from the warehouses at the city docks and for taking on goods from the side of ships in order to convey them to Avonside for transference to store or truck. A covered dock 160ft by 50ft was at the wharf. At the MR's King's Wharf, Redcliff Street, were cellars or caves hewn out of the red sandstone and used for the storage of up to 8,000 barrels of non-inflammable oils, wax etc. Grain, flour, sugar and such commodities were accepted for conveyance by barge to rail at Avonside in precisely the same manner as at stations, electric, steam and hydraulic cranes there quickly loading or discharging barges into or out of railway trucks. Today Avonside Wharf deals with

cement and molasses. When most of the former Midland line out of Bristol closed on 1 February 1970, a new chord line was opened from Lawrence Hill to give access to the wharf. Because of the curvature, only an engine of the '03' class can shunt the yard.

In 1974 a Freightliner depot was set up on the site of the former up yard at West Depot. Daily through Freightliners run to and from Manchester and Glasgow, the two portions being combined Bristol-Birmingham. At Glasgow containers can be transferred for Edinburgh or Aberdeen, and at Manchester to Newcastle or Ireland. Freightliners are not normally run Bristol-London as up to 150 miles the system is hardly competitive, but over 200 miles it certainly is. Extra Freightliners are laid on for special traffic, an example being meat and butter from Tilbury to Bristol. As Bristol is one of the smaller Freightliner depots and maintenance would be expensive, the crane is contract hired.

Wagon repair shops for the area are at Barton Hill. Originally MR and GWR, the intervening wall was only breached in 1962. Four stone trains come in weekly for preventive maintenance (a total of 120 wagons) plus about 40 other wagons. The Dutch-barn like Preventive Maintenance Shed was built in 1975 over two roads (the wall of the old broad gauge locomotive turntable pit being discovered when digging its foundations), one of which has an inspection pit built in 1958 for dmus and later used by the 'Bristol Pullman'. Intermediate repairs are also undertaken but general repairs are usually carried out at the main works. Porters' barrows and

Left: Avonside Wharf, June 1898.   *NRM*

Above: Lawrence Hill, view north, 21 August 1980.   *Author*

Right: Royal Mail container being loaded on wagon,
Freightliner Depot, 29 July 1980.   *Author*

platform seats are repaired. The shunting engine working
at Kingsland Road from 06.00 to 22.00 shunts Barton
Hill wagon works at night, after which the points are
locked and any wagons which need moving are pushed
by hand.

In 1851 two Quakers, Albert Fry and John Fowler
established themselves as agricultural implement
manufacturers and wheelwrights. Fowler left and later set
up his famous firm at Leeds. Albert's cousin Theodore
took the vacant partnership, their products including
furniture vans designed to fit on a railway truck. In 1866
Theodore left and the Bristol Wagon Works Co Ltd was
formed to take over the business with Albert Fry as
managing director. With the object of expanding business
by building railway rolling stock, a new factory was built
at Lawrence Hill beside the MR with a siding leading to
the works. In 1889 when it employed about 1,000 men,
the firm became the Bristol Wagon & Carriage Works Co
Ltd. Although some of the company's products were
bought by British railways, most were exported. Coach
bodies were built for Taff Vale and Great Northern steam

railmotors, some of the power units being supplied by the Avonside Engine Co Ltd. During World War 1 the company concentrated entirely on producing military material including rolling stock for the railways in France and narrow gauge trench lines. In 1920 the company was purchased by the Leeds Forge Co Ltd and the Newlay Wheel Co Ltd, but in 1923 Cammell, Laird Co Ltd took over the Leeds company and closed the Bristol works, the 13-acre site being bought by the Bristol Tramways & Carriage Co Ltd.

Above left: Trade card: GWR 0-6-0 shunting furniture vans at Clifton Down c1900.   *P.G. Davey*

Left: Wagon repairs, Barton Hill, 31 July 1980.   *Author*

Above: Wagon hoist, Barton Hill, 31 July 1980. Vans stand on former LMS down main line.   *Author*

Right: Barton Hill wagon works – exhauster for testing vacuum, 31 July 1980.   *Author*

The Motive Power Scene

The first locomotive to enter Bristol did so in 1835, five years before the GWR arrived in the city. Details are vague, but it was a small locomotive and the colliery proprietors said that they were trying to make do until '. . . we can get some proper sized steam carriages on the Rail Road similar to those in use at the Welsh Collieries, Iron Works and elsewhere'. A letter in the Ashton Court Collection written by Sir John Smyth to E. F. Colston on 23 February 1835 explained that following a modification to increase its speed so that it could make daily two trips instead of one over the Bristol & Gloucestershire line, Bond & Winwood's steam carriage exploded sending parts 300yd away. Its steam was 'generated in tubes, not in the boiler, to render it more safe'.

When the line was taken over by the Bristol & Gloucester Railway, the tender of a Bristol firm, Stothert, Slaughter & Co was accepted to work seven trains each way for £18,500 annually and in addition to providing the locomotives and rolling stock, the company maintained the line. This meant that the BGR avoided an outlay for repair shops, carriage sheds, engine sheds and coke ovens. In May 1844 Stothert, Slaughter & Co sought permission from the GWR to erect and paint the BGR carriages in Bristol station and give the locomotives trial runs on GWR metals. The locomotives built by the firm were of a design obtained from Bury, Curtis & Kennedy of Liverpool. They were 2-2-2s with inside bar frames, D-shaped fireboxes and weighed 18ton in working order. They were named:

No 4 *Bristol*
No 5 *Gloucester*
No 6 *Berkeley*
No 7 *Wickwar*
No 8 *Cheltenham*
No 9 *Stroud*

No 7 as MR No 463 was wrecked when its boiler exploded on 8 January 1853, but the others were made redundant when the MR went over to narrow gauge, were sold to Thomas Brassey in 1855-7 and were used by him and later the LSWR on the North Devon Railway. For BGR goods traffic, Stothert & Co built two 0-6-0s and three 2-4-0s. Locomotive running costs worked out at 11½d a mile, the same as the GWR, but the GWR ran heavier trains. The MR bought the locomotives from Stothert, Slaughter & Co in July 1845. J.E. McConnell, the Birmingham & Bristol locomotive superintendent, giving evidence before the Gauge Commission, said that

one of Slaughter's largest goods engines, with the assistance of a pilot engine up the incline to Staple Hill, hauled a gross load of 235 tons and covered the 37.5 miles to Gloucester in 4hr 13min including four stops. In 1846 Sharp Bros were given the contract to build a broad gauge engine for £3,000. In April 1847 Matthew Kirtley, locomotive superintendent of the MR, amended the order to four broad gauge convertible engines (Nos 66-9) and these were the first such engines to be built. In October 1853 the Midland Locomotive Committee instructed W.H. Barlow, the company's chief engineer, to adapt Bristol running shed to take narrow gauge engines and this gauge was extended to Bristol 1 June 1854 and from this date standard Midland engines were able to use the line.

No express engines were stabled at Bristol until the turn of the century, principal trains being worked by Derby and Saltley engines, mainly the latter. From 1854 until 1870 Kirtley 6ft 8in 2-2-2s Nos 120-9 worked expresses from Bristol to Birmingham when, as a result of enginemen sending a deputation to Kirtley complaining that singles were incapable of working heavy trains over the steeply graded line, they were replaced by 2-4-0s Nos 820-9. In turn, these were succeeded in 1880 by the Johnson '1282' class 2-4-0s, Nos 1282-96 still working the line in 1919. In 1892 4-2-2 singles worked Derby to Bristol but were replaced by 4-4-0s a few years later, though until the mid-1920s they could still be seen as train engines on reliefs as well as in use as pilots and Nos 673/9 ended their days on locals to Gloucester. 4-4-0 Compounds and the '990' class did not penetrate to Bristol before the Grouping and the heaviest duties on the 'Devonian' and Newcastle mail were performed by Class 3 4-4-0s, while lighter expresses were handled by those of Class 2. Compounds appeared in 1924, the post-Grouping series being run in on Derby to Bristol expresses and shortly after this Nos 1028-32 were shedded at Bristol. 'Jubilees' appeared in 1934 and gradually took over the heaviest trains, while during World War 2 'Patriots', the first of which had appeared on the line in 1931, were given the heaviest train, the 7.40am from Bristol, always of 15 bogies. Class 5s did

Top right: Up 'Devonian' leaving Temple Meads c1938 hauled by Compound No 1027.   *NRM*

Right: No 45682 *Trafalgar* passing Barrow Road MPD, 20 July 1953, with 10.13am Bristol-Newcastle.   *D.T. Flook*

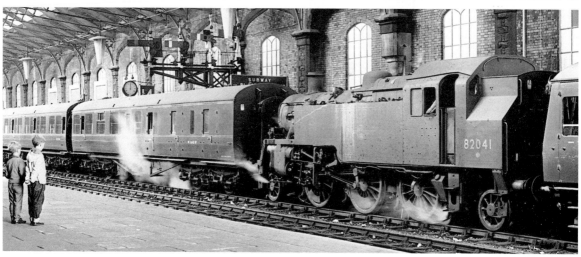

excellent work on Derby expresses handling 12-coach trains while several Caprotti 'Black Fives' worked to Derby running freely, but never having the 'guts' of a piston valve engine in getting away from a stop or climbing. 'Crabs' were used on passenger trains and 'Royal Scot' No 46120 *Royal Inniskilling Fusilier* appeared in February 1949. In 1941 rebuilt SER 'F1' class 4-4-0s worked trains from Bristol to Gloucester while in November 1941 the SR lent Drummond 'K10' mixed traffic 4-4-0s Nos 135/7/8 and 388/9 to the LMS, Nos 137/8 being shedded at Gloucester and Nos 135,388/9 at Bristol. No 135 tended to work the Thornbury goods while Nos 388/9 shunted or worked local goods. They returned to the SR by March 1945. Eastern Region 'B1' 4-6-0s came in 1958 especially on the 12.48pm from York which introduced 'V2' 2-6-2 No 60954 on 16 November 1959. In January 1963 No 60945 arrived, but someone realised it was not cleared for the route and it was returned via Didcot on the night freight to Woodford Halse. Eastern Region engines of the 'K1', 'K3', 'O1' and 'O4' classes are also recorded as visiting the Bristol area. LMS engines worked through to Weston super Mare on pre-World War 2 excursions from the Midlands, while in the latter days of steam, ER 'B1s' worked through Weston super Mare-Sheffield trains on Saturdays.

Top left: ER 'B1' class No 61167 leaving Temple Meads with a Paignton to Bradford train, 17 August 1963. *H. Ballantyne*

Centre left: No 82041 at Temple Meads with the 12.12(SO) to Bath Green Park, 3 October 1964. *B. J. Ashworth*

Below: LMS banana train leaving Avonmouth Dock on 17 September 1929 hauled by '4F' 0-6-0 No 4278. *NRM*

Below right: No 03.382 shunting at Lawrence Hill, 21 August 1980. *Author*

At the turn of the century 0-4-4Ts Nos 1274-81 were shedded at Bristol to work Clifton Down and Bath trains, from the 1930s being assisted by a Class 3P 2-6-2T. During 1947 Johnson 0-4-4Ts were mainly replaced by Stanier '2P' 0-4-4Ts, only to be ousted two years later by Class 2MTs of the '412xx' series aided by Standard Class 3MTs of the same wheel arrangement. On 19 February 1953 ex-GWR railcar No W37, coach No 6582 and No W38 ran from Bristol to Bath Green Park on a gauging trip. From the beginning of the winter timetable single and twin railcars worked some trains and, when unavailable, ex-GWR 2-6-2Ts or 'Panniers' took over the same roster. 'Westerns', 'Peaks', 'Hymeks' and 'Warships' also appeared on trains to Green Park, though BR dmus were extremely rare.

Until the appearance of the Stanier '8Fs', goods trains were worked by 0-6-0s including Avonmouth to London banana trains via Broom Junction, the Stratford on Avon & Midland Junction line. Somerset & Dorset 2-8-0s worked freight trains from Avonmouth and Westerleigh to Bath, while the occasional Beyer-Garratt or LNWR 0-8-0 put in an appearance on trains from the north. From March 1950 a Garratt from Toton worked daily to Westerleigh, spent the night at Barrow Road and returned with the early morning freight or empties the next day. In 1954 ex-Barry Railway 0-6-2T GWR No 285 withdrawn the previous year, was in use as a stationary boiler at Barrow Road. The sharply curved Avonside Wharf line required MR 0-4-0STs and in post-Grouping years LYR 'Pugs' put in an appearance. In 1961 the duties of Nos 51217/8 were taken over by 204hp diesel shunters Nos D2134/5 later classified as the '03' class. The first diesel shunter on ex-LMS lines at Bristol was No 13187 which arrived at Barrow Road 1 June 1958 and began work on 2 June.

For the opening of the GWR between Bristol and Bath on 31 August 1840, six of Daniel Gooch's new engines

were ready: *Arrow* and *Dart* had been built at Bristol by Stothert, Slaughter & Co while *Fire Ball*, *Spit Fire* and *Lynx* of the 'Firefly' class and *Meridian* of the 'Sun' class were made by various other manufacturers. *Meridian* was rumoured to have come in parts by barge and been assembled in Saltford Tunnel. The first engine shed, a parallelogram in shape, was a small three road affair accommodating 15 locomotives and situated on the north side of the line near the site of the later South Wales Junction, while opposite were coke ovens, with a weekly capacity of about 450ton, supplying all GWR engines with smokeless fuel and superseding the original small establishment at West Drayton. Coking coal from the Rhondda Valley travelled by sea from Cardiff to Bristol, there being of course no rail communication at that date.

The B&E at first was worked by the GWR, but in 1849 its financial position was such that it became completely independent and had its own engines and rolling stock. Locomotive workshops were opened at Bristol in January 1852 on the site of the present Bath Road diesel depot, were considerably extended in September 1854, turned out their first completed locomotive in 1859 and built 34 more during the next 16 years, a total of 23 broad gauge, 10 standard and two 3ft gauge. The B&E

*Left: **Argus** of the 'Fire Fly' class which worked passenger trains to Paddington.*   *Bristol Museum*

*Below left: **Great Britain** at Bristol GWR loco shed.*   *LPC*

*Below: **GWR No 2002**, formerly B&E No 40 built at Bristol in 1873.*   *LPC*

having a relatively short main line of only 76 miles tended to use tank engines, the most impressive examples being 4-2-4 express tank locomotives designed by James Pearson with 9ft driving wheels. 4-4-0STs were also used for main line passenger duties, other tank engines being of the 2-2-2T, 2-2-2WT, 0-6-0ST and 0-4-0WT wheel arrangement, the latter designed for shunting. Tender engines comprised those of the 4-2-2, 0-6-0 and 2-4-0 types.

Practically all classes of GWR engines have appeared at Bristol, including the de Glehn Atlantics. Circa 1905 *La France* left Exeter with 12 corridors – 330 tons behind the tender – ran 75.5 miles to Bristol start-to-stop in 77.5min, an average speed of 62.5mph then it ran on to London with the same load, 118.5 miles in 118min. Another interesting engine was the Pacific No 111 *The Great Bear* whose weight limited it to the London to Bristol line on which it worked both expresses and fast fitted freights, the latter also being worked by 2-8-0s of the '47xx' class handling up to 70 vehicles. Tank engines too were used on this route and in 1907 it is recorded that the 5.30am newspaper and mail train from Paddington was worked to Bristol by a 4-4-2T equipped with water pick up apparatus, arriving at 8.28, returning on the 9.35am from Bristol arriving Paddington 12.20. In 1911 two-car railmotors worked 14 trips each way between Temple Meads and Clifton Down, but were not used through Clifton Down tunnel or on the Hotwells line. In the 1930s Drummond 'D15' 4-4-0s ran from Salisbury to Bristol and back every evening, while for a period 'U' class 2-6-0s worked through regularly on a Saturday and returned on Sunday while Bulleid Pacifics were seen on postwar football specials. In 1934 some surplus South

Below: Up railmotor No 58 at Pill c1910.   *M.J. Tozer collection*

Bottom: '2201' class No 2217 stands at Stapleton Road with a down stopping train consisting of 4-wheel coaches, c1905. The photographer was killed in World War 1.   *J. C. Young*

Right: No 3407 *Madras* shunting horse box and officers' coach at Temple Meads, 1933.   *NRM*

Bottom right: ROD No 3034 stands over the ashpit outside St Philip's Marsh shed, 19 August 1951.   *H. Ballantyne*

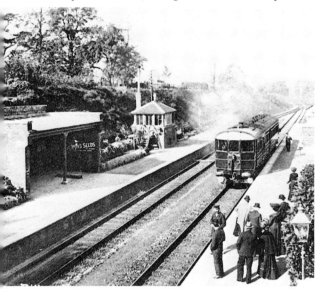

Left: No 5104 outside St Philip's Marsh shed, 6 December 1959.   *H. Ballantyne*

Below left: 'Black Five' No 45265 and ex-GWR No 6399 at Temple Meads, 14 June 1958.   *R.E. Toop*

Right: 'Star' class No 4056 *Princess Margaret* at Temple Meads, 31 August 1957.   *H. Ballantyne*

Centre right: 2-8-0T No 5215 on freight train to Filton Junction near Stapleton Road, May 1959.   *P. Ransome-Wallis*

Below: No 4358 following war damage at Bristol.   *BR*

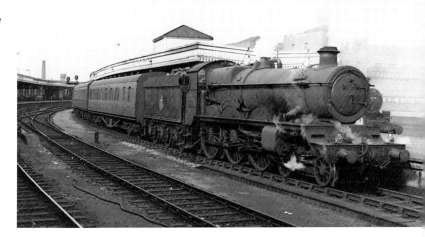

Top: Gas turbine No 18000 with Bristol-Paddington express. *M.E.J. Deane*

Above: Gas turbine No 18100 with up express to Paddington, 22 August 1953. *R. E. Toop*

Left: 'Britannia' class No 70022 *Tornado* with Plymouth train, 2 June 1953. *R.E. Toop*

Above right: Sea Mills: first day of driver training with three-car dmu, September 1958. *M. Farr*

Wales 2-8-0Ts were converted to 2-8-2Ts carrying a larger bunker almost equalling the coal capacity of a tender engine so they could undertake main line coal traffic working and some were used between Bristol and Salisbury.

Between August 1940 and March 1941 12 GWR locomotives were damaged in air raids on Bristol. During World War 2 trains of USA 2-8-0s passed through on their way to Swindon and after being checked over were seen on freights as were GWR built LMS '8Fs' and the WD Austerities. During this period local passenger services were worked by '45xx' 2-6-2Ts, 'Pannier' tanks or diesel railcars. Gas turbine No 18000 made its appearance on Paddington trains in 1949 followed three years later by No 18100. The first BR Standard class to appear was the 'Britannia' and was followed by most of the other classes. BR dmus were first used at Bristol on 18 August 1958 when two Gloucester Railway Carriage & Wagon Works W55018/9 were used on alternate days on the Clifton Down line. By 3 September, the Bristol allocation of Derby-built suburban 3-car units, Class 116, began to arrive and these soon took over the training trips. The first stage of Bristol suburban dieselisation was introduced on 5 October 1958 and Stage Two came into force on 17 November. Dmus allocated to Bristol for the period ending December 1958 were 56 motor cars. On 6 April 1959 stopping trains on Swindon to Weston super Mare and Bristol, Westbury and Weymouth lines were dieselised. A little later 'Warships', 'Westerns', 'Hymeks' and Class 47s appeared on expresses and in 1968-9 Paddington to Bristol was the hunting ground of No D0280 *Falcon* which in the author's experience was an excellent engine and could be relied on to bring its train in on time.

Class 50s made redundant by London Midland Region West Coast electrification superseded Class 47s and 'Westerns' on Bristol-Paddington trains on 6 May 1974. Many failures occurred initially because on Brunel's main line the locomotives were having to run at their full speed for longer than they had been required to do before.

Eventually matters were cured by altering the armatures and by 1978 the Western Region had succeeded in improving them to the reliability of the Class 47s. Meanwhile following trial runs between Bristol and London on 16-19 December 1974, IC125 No 252.001 appeared on some trains in 1975, a regular service beginning in the spring of 1977. Numbers in use increased and since 1976 patronage of Inter-City trains from the Bristol area has risen by nearly 18% a rise due mainly to the impact the IC125 has had on the public. IC125s are put to far more intensive use than any other BR diesel traction unit and average 750 miles a day in revenue earning service, half of this being at over 100mph. Between May 1980 and May 1981 insufficient IC125s were available for a full Penzance to Paddington IC125 service to be run, so locomotive and coach working was reintroduced for some Bristol to Paddington fast trains stopping only at Bath and Reading. There were 12 of these locomotive-hauled trains which were limited to 100mph and eight air-braked coaches. They tended to arrive early on their timetable which allowed them a generous 12-20min longer than the IC125s, which were retained for the stopping services as they could accelerate faster.

The Bristol Port Railway & Pier possessed only two locomotives, 0-4-2Ts of the Bury or Fairburn type whose early history is obscure; they were probably St Helen's Railway No 4 *Hercules* and No 23 *Hero* built 1856 and 1853-4. On the BPRP they had a livery of dark green and were not fitted with a vacuum brake. They were hauled to the line through the streets of Bristol by 30 MR horses. Small repairs were undertaken at the company's locomotive depot at Shirehampton, but they had to be sent to Peckett's for more extensive work and a replacement hired from the MR. 0-6-0WTs Nos 2002 and 2013 are known to have been borrowed and as the latter was being hauled on a cart along the newly made Perry Road one Whit Saturday, it became embedded in soft ground and required 60 horses to pull it out. Fortunately it arrived in time for working the Bank

Holiday Monday traffic. When the GWR and MR bought the line, the 0-4-2Ts were condemned and replaced with locomotives from GWR stock.

The first GWR locomotive shed at Bristol was on the north side of the line east of Temple Meads near the site of the later South Wales Junction and was a three-road shed, a four-road building being added. Bath Road shed (BRD in the GWR code, 82A in BR code) was originally a six-road B&E depot set diagonally beside the locomotive works. In latter broad gauge days it was mixed gauge. The complex was rebuilt in 1934 when lines either side of Temple Meads were quadrupled. The main shed, 210ft by 167ft with 10 roads, was built approximately on the site of the locomotive works, constructed of bricks and had a slated roof with the usual raised central louvred and glazed vent to each bay. Beside it was a three-road repair shop, 170ft by 50ft, steel framed with brick walls and a slated roof, a coal stage surmounted by a 135,000gal water tank separating the two buildings. The water came from Fox's Wood pumping station which supplied St Philip's Marsh shed as well as the water troughs. Originally lifted from the river by a steam pump, an electric pump was fitted latterly, a bell ringing at Bath Road when failure occurred. Fish were sometimes sucked through the 15in pipes, the author having it on good authority that an eel spent three years in the water tank of a shunting engine. On the east side of the Bath Road complex was a gas works supplying fuel for lighting buildings and yards. Gas was piped to Marsh Pond, Dr Day's and Malago Vale for coaches, boys being employed to 'gas up' coaches and having to endure the smell clinging to their hands and clothes. Rail tank wagons were sent to stations in the area to replenish

Above: **BPRP No 1.** *Dr A.J.G. Dickens' collection*

Above right: Inkermann **outside the GWR shed, with Temple Meads in the background.** *LPC*

Right: **Former B&E locomotive factory c1930, with the Bristol Avoiding Line at the foot of the picture.** *M. J. Tozer collection*

coach gas tanks. The shed closed to steam on 12 September 1960, the locomotives being transferred to St Philip's Marsh and Barrow Road. The depot was rebuilt at a cost of over £700,000 and opened on 18 June 1962 as a diesel depot with six roads servicing about 140 diesels. One of the features of the depot in the 1960s was that it had an annual open day when, in addition to its usual locomotives, interesting engines were brought from elsewhere. Circa 1964 the depot had difficulty in recruiting more than 75% of the maintenance staff needed because of the attraction of the local aircraft industry. Today the depot has three sections:

1 A three-road running or 'daily' shed for fuelling and very light maintenance. At the time of writing (1980) this shed is to be lengthened so that it can contain a three-car dmu set.
2 A light maintenance shed with six roads, used for more thorough examinations and for work which takes too long to be satisfactorily undertaken in the running shed where a locomotive stays for only a short period.
3 A heavy lifting shop with overhead gantry crane and used for major repairs of locomotives and IC125 power cars.

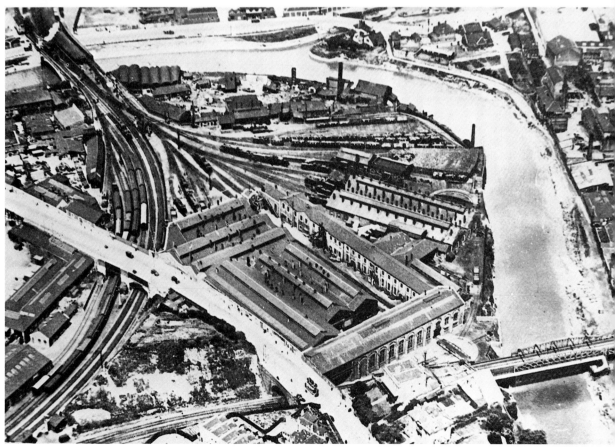

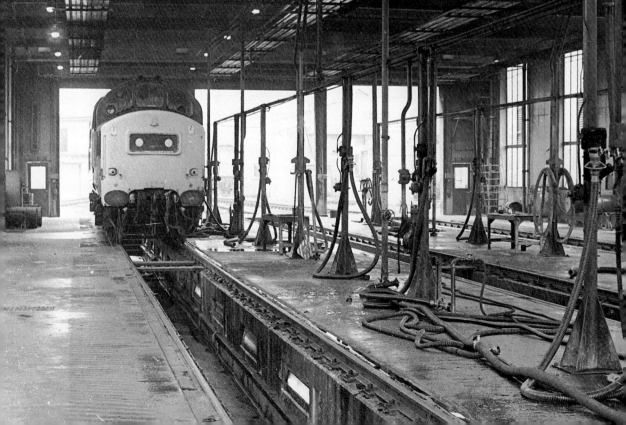

In the yard between the running and light maintenance shed operated by photo-electric cells is an automatic washing machine which cleans an engine with detergent and rinses it. Beside the running shed is an apparatus for cleaning locomotive underframes. There is a 146ton Rapier 65ft turntable, which is also part of an escape road from the shed to the relief line to be used if the main exit became blocked. Fuel oil is kept in three 135,000gal tanks. The area where locomotives are stored between the heavy lifting shop and the river is still called the 'coal yard'. In 1965 1,250 staff were employed (including Marsh Junction) for train running, servicing and maintenance, of which just over 800 were for train running purposes. Drivers at the depot required a route knowledge to London, Plymouth, Cardiff, Hereford, Derby, Salisbury and Weymouth. By 1969 staff had been reduced to 1,000, just over 600 being for train running. 1980 figures show 300 drivers, 110 second men, 29 'M' turns and 180 guards. A drivers' classroom is situated in

Left: **Bath Road MPD, 9 July 1960. The repair shop is on the left of the water tower.**   *H. Ballantyne*

Below left: **Inside the 'daily' shed Bath Road, 29 July 1980.** *Author*

Right: **Paper sacks of dry sand at the 'daily' shed, 29 July 1980.**   *Author*

Below: **No 253.005 in heavy lifting shop, Bath Road, 29 July 1980.**   *Author*

Top: Underframe cleaning pit, Bath Road, 29 July 1980.   *Author*

Above: Fuel tankers being discharged, Bath Road, 29 July 1980.   *Author*

Left: Large snow plough, Bath Road, 29 July 1980.   *Author*

the administrative block and another in a converted coach. Between the depot and the station is the Locomotive Test Centre built basically to improve the Class 50s. When engines were on test their traction motors were disconnected and the power taken to the test centre. In the depot yard is a 145ton steam crane and a 75ton diesel crane to cover the area Tiverton-Bromsgrove, Warminster and Didcot. Other equipment includes two large snowploughs which run outside two Class 50s; four Class 31 and 37 locomotives are fitted with small ploughs.

St Philip's Marsh depot (SPM, later 82B) was opened on 9 July 1910 and basically supplied locomotives for freight working, while Bath Road concentrated on passenger engines. The Marsh did, however, provide power in the form of 'Halls' and 'Granges' for the many Saturday north to west trains using the avoiding line, engines or crews being changed near the shed. Situated south of the relief line it was the second largest depot on the GWR. 28 roads radiated from each of the two turntables while adjacent was a two road repair shop, later having a steel framed corrugated extension added for the maintenance of GWR railcars by AEC fitters, GWR cleaners wiping the bodywork with cleaning oil. The main building, 246ft by 364ft, was of brick standing on concrete piles as it was on made ground. Below the water tank which held 145,000gal was a two-road coal stage. The manually operated table used for larger engines was in the roundhouse furthest from the avoiding line, while the electric table for smaller engines was in the other building. The depot closed 13 June 1964 when the few remaining engines were transferred to Barrow Road, the shed being demolished the following February and a wholesale fruit and vegetable market erected.

In 1949 Nos 2031 and 2035 were used on the Harbour lines and Canon's Marsh, but were replaced by the '16xx' class, a modern edition of the '2021' class. '66xx' 0-6-2Ts were used on Stoke Gifford to Avonmouth transfer trips. BR Standard Class 9s and ex-LMS '8Fs' appeared at the Marsh in the late 1950s. The first diesel-electric shunter at Bristol was GWR No 2 which arrived in January 1949 as No 15100, the only GWR engine to be renumbered under the BR scheme; No 15107 arrived new in November. By February 1954 Nos 13000/3 had arrived and in September 1956 ex-Southern Region shunter No 15230 appeared. Twelve diesel shunters arrived at the Marsh in 1958 and displaced 'Pannier' tanks.

Barrow Road (MR code 8, LMS 22A and 82E in the WR) was a brick built roundhouse but, unlike the GWR sheds, it had a modern coaling tower. In 1935 LMS motive power depots were reorganised into locomotive supply concentration and garage schemes, Bristol becoming a main, or concentration depot, with Gloucester, Bath/Radstock, Templecombe, Highbridge, Tewkesbury and Wells as garage depots. The object of the scheme was to effect economies by reducing the necessity of stocking so many parts at smaller depots. The district locomotive superintendent had his office at Bristol. The depot was well-equipped with a wheel drop

pit, a wheel lathe, two sheer legs, an ash disposal plant and two turntables. It closed on 16 November 1965 and did not indicate the complete cessation of steam in Bristol, because steam-hauled freight trains Birmingham-Bristol continued until August 1966, but by October Barrow Road shed was demolished.

The four-road Marsh Junction dmu depot brought into use on 23 February 1959 also serviced D6XX and D8XX diesel-hydraulics until Bath Road reopened as a diesel depot. Marsh Junction's 1965 allocation was 32 cross-country trains, 12 suburban, four single cars and one Pullman. It was closed on 18 May 1970 so that it could be used for maintaining the Civil Engineer's plant, dmus being maintained at Bath Road but still fuelled at Marsh Junction. In the summer of 1973 when Mk IID coaches were used on Bristol to London services, maintenance of their 1,000V electric heating had to be carried out under cover, Roads 3 & 4 of the former dmu depot being utilised for this and 1 & 2 for the maintenance of the Civil Engineer's yellow track machines, Road 1 being shortened to allow space to repair vehicles such as bulldozers and Iron Fairies. Half of Bristol's coach maintenance staff is at Marsh Junction and half at Malago Vale.

A 700ft long three-road IC125 maintenance depot opened on the site of the former cattle pens at St Philip's Marsh in September 1975 at a cost of £1.5million. Fluorescent strip lighting was used throughout the shed and the white floor was coated with a paint which resisted oil impregnation. This gave a light and clean appearance to the depot and encouraged staff to keep their footwear clean and not spread dirt through the trains. As the shed is purpose-built, at the point where power cars stop for diesel fuel, oil and coolant, a grid is placed in the floor for spillage to run through. The concept of the shed is that the whole of the IC125 is serviced in one place at one time – normally locomotives and coaches are serviced in different places. Four Matterson 20ton SWL jacks lift a power car for bogie changing or maintenance, the jacks being designed so that they can be moved round the shed by fork lift. 1.5ton SWL cranes are provided at each end of the shed for removing small items from power cars. Two Worthington-Simpson Type 3DPM4 pumps offload oil fuel which is stored in 90,000gal bulk storage tanks and 7,500gal of lubricating oil. Outside is a Smith Bros & Webb washing plant. The former St Philip's Marsh good yard, now renamed Victoria Sidings, and with eight roads and a cripples' siding, is used for overnight stabling of IC125s. Nineteen sets, the odd numbers from Nos 253.001-37, receive maintenance at Bristol. A special shunter, No 08.483 with buckeye coupler and air brake, is kept for moving IC125 power cars between the depot and the Heavy Lifting Shed, Bath Road.

The other major locomotive owner in the Bristol area is the Port of Bristol Authority, though with a severe reduction in rail traffic to and from the docks, the stud is a shadow of what it was. At one time the PBA maintained a fleet of about 20 locomotives for shunting over 70 miles of track at Avonmouth and 10 miles at Portishead. The

Above: Interior of St Philip's Marsh MPD, Large side. From left to right: No 5050 *Earl of St Germans;* No 4701 and No 1020 *County of Monmouth.*
H. Ballantyne

Above right: No 2070 at Canon's Marsh. *M.E.J. Deane*

Right: St Philip's Marsh MPD, Small side. No 6656, No 9011 and No 4624. E.D. Bruton

Far right: Barrow Road MPD: a 'Black Five', No 45662 *Kempenfelt,* and No 42890. *Ivo Peters*

0-6-0STs were built locally by Fox Walker's, Avonside and Peckett's and named after local places or port officials. In 1950 an 0-4-0 diesel was purchased from Hudswell, Clarke & Co Ltd and over the next 10 years a total of two 0-4-0 and 16 0-6-0 diesel-mechanical shunters were purchased from this firm, followed in 1963-5 by nine Sentinel (Shrewsbury) Ltd/Rolls-Royce Ltd 0-6-0 diesel-hydraulic shunters, the last steam locomotive being withdrawn on 6 August 1965, eight days after delivery of the final diesel-hydraulic. The PBA found diesel traction advantageous giving a higher availability, lower fuel cost and less fire risk, the latter an important factor in docks. All the diesel-mechanical

Above: Locos on shed at Barrow Road include '5F' 2-6-0 No 42764, ex-S&D 0-4-0T Sentinel No 47190, '3F' No 43427 and GWR 2-6-0 No 6350. *Ivo Peters*

Left: No 73003, No 48409 and steam crane at Barrow Road MPD. *R. E. Toop*

Above right: Ashes being disposed from No 48763 at Barrow Road MPD on 16 August 1950. *Author*

Right: Marsh Junction Depot, Civil Engineering repair side-tamper, 31 July 1980. *Author*

shunters have been disposed of and today eight Sentinel/Rolls-Royce locomotives cope with traffic, usually only two or three in use daily and worked in rotation to keep them in running order. Locomotives are maintained at Avonmouth in a four-road shed built in 1950, with a one-road service bay, heavy repairs being undertaken in the PBA workshops. The locomotive depot at Portishead was closed in 1970 and since then any locomotives used there have been stored in the open. Each PBA engine has a crew of four: driver, fireman, shunter and pointsman, crews cleaning and maintaining their own engine. At one time three shifts were worked, but today the hours are 08.00 to 17.00, any extra being covered by overtime. To speed communication and make working more efficient, in 1975 the locomotives were fitted with radio to obviate the difficulty of contacting a driver by phone. Steam locomotives were in a green livery as were most of the early diesels, but the Sentinels were given a new livery of Oxford blue.

Locomotive building was an important Bristol industry, in fact more engines were built at Bristol than at Derby, Darlington or Doncaster. Bristol built 24.8% of British broad gauge locomotives and from 1864 to 1881, one in nine of the locomotives built in Britain was made at Bristol. In 1837 Henry Stothert, a Bath engineer who expanded to Bristol, founded the Avonside Ironworks at St Philip's, Edward Slaughter, an assistant engineer to Brunel, joined the company in 1841. Locomotive construction began in 1840, engines being supplied to most major railway companies, a high proportion going to broad gauge lines such as the GWR, B&E and Bristol & Gloucester. A new partnership, Slaughter, Gruning & Co formed in 1856, was dissolved in 1864 when the firm was registered as the Avonside Engine Company Limited – only the second locomotive firm to become a public limited company under the terms of the 1862 Companies Act. In 1865 Avonside built a GWR 'Hawthorn' class 2-4-0 and named it *Slaughter,* and, so the story goes, one of the Great Western directors strolling up to look at the engine hauling his train was horrified to see its name, had it removed and *Avonside* substituted. In 1871 the first of a hundred or so Fairlie Patent locomotives left Avonside works and additionally about 30 single-ended types were built. In the mid-1870s Avonside was employing a workforce of 800-900 and building about 50 locomotives annually, well over half of them for export to India, South

America and Australasia, but by the end of the decade the world market for main line locomotives had become highly competitive and this, together with a world wide trade recession, forced the Bristol firm into a final voluntary liquidation in 1881 after a brief period of recapitalisation following a collapse two years before.

Fox, Walker & Co established the Atlas Locomotive Works in Deep Pit Road, St George the same year that the Avonside Engine Co Ltd was formed. Access to this factory was by way of a colliery branch line from Kingswood Junction. The firm specialised in four and six-wheeled industrial saddle tank engines in addition to locomotives for the new narrow gauge railways which were being laid in many countries. The largest Fox, Walker engines were nine 0-6-0STs built 1874-5 for the Somerset & Dorset Railway. Some 400 locomotives were built before the firm failed in December 1878 as a result of costly and unsuccessful experimental work with street tramway engines and a complex patent machine – Handyside's Steep Gradient Locomotive. Edwin Walker, having salvaged patterns and spares from the firm, leased a part of the old Avonside Ironworks and in 1882 began to trade as the Avonside Engine Company. He continued the Fox, Walker policy of building industrial tank engines and narrow gauge locomotives for export. In 1904 a new partnership was formed and a modern factory erected adjacent to Fishponds station, locomotive building commencing there in 1905. The firm became a limited company in 1909, this time a private one, and survived until the slump of the 1930s brought voluntary

Above: **PBA Avonside 0-6-0ST** *Francis* **at Avonmouth.** *A.H. Hack collection*

Above right: **PBA Fox Walker 0-6-0ST** *Bristol* **at Avonmouth.** *Port of Bristol Authority*

Right: **PBA 0-6-0 No 34 at Avonmouth, 11 April 1980.** *Author*

liquidation. The works closed in 1934, the goodwill being taken over by the Hunslet Engine Co Ltd, the factory being bought by Parnall & Co Ltd. Meanwhile the Atlas Locomotive Works had been taken over by Thomas Peckett who formed a partnership, Thomas Peckett & Sons, in 1880. His building policy was similar to Walker's in that industrial locomotives, substantially to Walker's design, were built. Peckett's, however, never established themselves in the narrow gauge export market. The firm became a private limited company in 1914 and lasted until 1958 when it was taken over by the Reed Crane & Hoist Co Ltd.

The Bristol City Museum has preserved 0-6-0STs by each of the three builders:

Loco & Owner	Builder	Year	Where Preserved
Mountain Ash Colliery	Fox, Walker	1874	Bristol Suburban Railway, Bitton
PBA No S3 *Portbury*	Avonside	1917	West Somerset Railway
PBA No S9 *Henbury*	Peckett	1937	Industrial Museum, Prince's Wharf, Bristol

The Bristol Suburban Railway Society also have two
other Bristol engines:
Imperial Smelting Works, Peckett 1918,
Aberthaw & Bristol Channel Portland Cement Co
Peckett 1924.

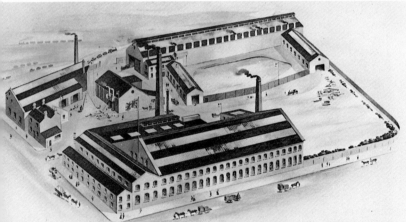

Above: GWR 'Hawthorn' class *Avonside* built by Avonside Engine Co Ltd. *LPC*

Left: Peckett's Atlas Locomotive Works. *Bristol Museum*

Below: Erecting shop at Peckett's Atlas Works. *Author's collection*

Passenger stations and goods sheds

Brunel's imposing Tudor style Bristol terminus, which matched many of the bridges and tunnels from Bath westwards, was built on a field called Temple Meads. Constructed on brick arches 15ft above ground level, it formed a parallelogram 408ft by 114ft. On the north and old departure side on the ground floor were the booking offices. Luggage was carried up in lifts, but passengers used stairs to reach the platforms. The walls were in Bath stone, while the impressive timber cantilever train shed roof had a span of 72ft unsupported by any cross tie or abutment, being carried on octagonal iron piers with four-centred arches. Each principal was formed of two frameworks like cranes, meeting in the centre of the roof, the weight being carried on the octagonal columns and the tail ends of the frames held down by the side walls. As the two frames did not press against each other where they met, there was no outward thrust. The octagonal piers were rather close to the edge of the platform and caused an awkward obstruction to passengers, but the difficulty was obviated when broad gauge was abolished and the platforms could be widened. The glazed roof had a length of 220ft and the platforms extended for a further 200ft. Beyond the train shed, very much like the nave of a church with the platforms as aisles, was the flat ceilinged chancel where locomotives were stored. Forsaking the Gothic, the ceiling was supported by closely spaced slender unembellished iron columns. Above and in front of this engine shed was the four-storey office block and it was not unknown for steam from engines to seep up through the floorboards.

The symmetrical Tudor facade facing Temple Gate had angle turrets and a centre oriel above which are the arms of the cities of Bristol and London adopted by the GWR for its own arms. Originally there were two flanking gateways, the departure side on the left having a clock, but the right gateway was removed, probably when the tram terminus along the southern wall of the train shed was electrified. The whole impression of the original station was that of a gentleman's country seat and would have boosted the confidence of nervous early travellers.

When the B&E opened in 1841 it used the GWR terminus at Bristol. This involved backing trains into or out of the station, and so, in 1845, it opened its own terminus at right angles to the east end of the GWR station. It was a simple wooden construction with overall roof, lacking the height of its nearby GWR counterpart. It spanned two platform roads and two centre roads for stabling coaches. Because of its construction and position near the cattle market, it was popularly known as the

Below: **Frontage of GWR terminus, Bristol.**   *Author*

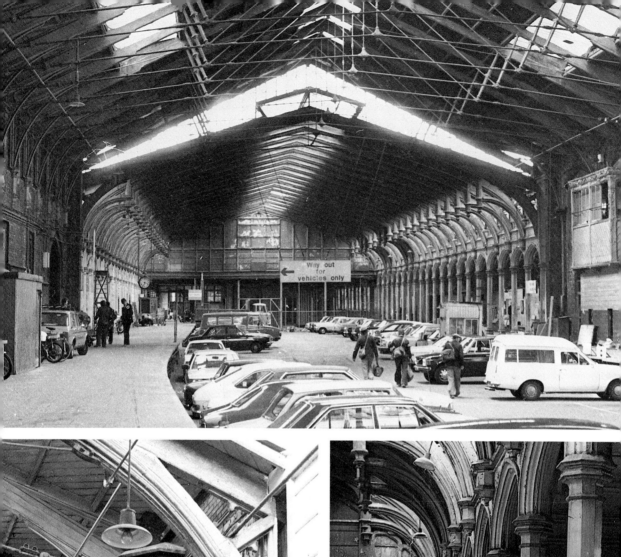

Left: Wyatt's (nearer) and Brunel's (beyond), train shed in use as car park, 30 May 1980.   *Author*

Below far left: Brunel and Wyatt beams in terminal train shed, 1 August 1980. *Author*

Below left: Wooden octagonal piers, Brunel train shed, 30 May 1980. *Author*

Right: Engine shed at terminal end of Brunel's train shed, 1 August 1980. *Author*

Below: B&E office block, 29 May 1980.   *Author*

'cow shed'. A double track curve linked the two railways and an 'express platform' was provided by the B&E on the up line, but used by both up and down expresses. This platform was not invariably used for such trains, as in 1862 the down 'Flying Dutchman' ran to the end of the curve and then backed into the B&E terminus. In 1852 the B&E were one better than the GWR for they opened a refreshment room at their station. The same year, work started on the new office block to the south of the station approach. Completed in October 1854 it was designed by F. C. Fripp whose initials are carried high on the north side of the building which is of symmetrical Jacobean design with shaped gables and twin towers with ogee caps. When the B&E became amalgamated with the GWR in 1876, the offices were taken over by the GWR's Bristol Operating Division. They now contain the West of England Divisional Control dealing with the area from Penzance to the Severn Tunnel, Challow and Salisbury.

In 1861 a plan backed by the GWR was put forward for extending the B&E, MR and GWR to a new central station in Queen Square, but this suggestion was rejected by a narrow majority of the city council, so the three companies fell back on the idea of building a new joint station at Temple Meads. It was certainly necessary: in 1863 only two platforms dealt with GWR trains running to London, Westbury and New Passage Pier and MR services to Birmingham. Temple Meads was becoming very congested, the *Bristol Times & Mirror* remarking:

'It would be difficult to find in all England a more rambling, ill-arranged and melancholy-looking group of buildings than those for the Midland, Great Western and Bristol & Exeter lines. The Midland and Great Western station makes a massive show outside; but the outside is delusive, for the accommodation provided by way of offices is of the smallest. It is really a punishment for a man to have to squeeze himself in among the crowds that assemble every day at the starting of almost every train, in front of a single pigeon-hole that is used for the issue of tickets and for a lady, the difficulty of getting a ticket must be something dreadful. The Bristol & Exeter is certainly a trifle better in this respect than the others, but not much.'

In 1865 the GWR, B&E and MR obtained an Act to build a new joint station, but because of disputes regarding the proportionate division of the cost, another six years passed before work was even begun and a further six was needed for the task to be completed. Meanwhile in 1871 a new thoroughfare, Victoria Street/Temple Street, was made to link the city with the joint station. The B&E terminus was demolished and a great curved train shed with a span of 125ft was built on the site of the former B&E express platform to cover the new platforms. Vernon & Evans of the Central Iron Works, Cheltenham were contractors for the metal work. Brunel's original train shed was lengthened in similar style to the original, though the roof supports were metal not wood and had thin ties. The enlarged station, V-shaped in plan, opened on 1 January 1878, had a fine rising approach road to an architecturally pleasing main entrance, with offices and a

100ft high clock tower of Draycot stone approximately on the site of the old B&E terminus. Sir Matthew Digby Wyatt, an old friend of Brunel who had assisted him with his 1854 Paddington station, was architect for the extension and his design blended with the original. Francis Fox of the B&E took his share in the scheme, the green and gold exterior canopy almost certainly being of his design, because it is virtually identical to the one he designed for Weston super Mare. Each company had its own booking hall within the Great Hall and passengers for the respective companies entered by separate doors, a scroll above each bearing the appropriate legend – the MR the left hand door, the B&E centre and the GWR the right. Inside the entrance doors can still be seen the pinewood porters' booths, but the imposing pine entrance doors were removed as they had to be left open and this caused the entrance hall to be cold and draughty in winter; they were replaced by glass swing doors. The first section of the new station opened on 6 July 1874. Access to the down platforms was by a road leading south of the B&E offices and passing under the line. The red brick walls of the interior of the curved train shed have been cleaned fairly recently and the effective black brick decoration at the top seen for the first time in many years.

The extended station had seven platforms and in the new train shed, counting from the east, were Nos 1 to 4, No 1, the down main, was 286yd long and Nos 2-4 were each of 143yd length, the island platform being mainly used for down MR trains and to facilitate interchange, enabling passengers to walk straight across the platform to the down GWR train. Platform 4 was the GWR up main; platforms 5 & 6 were the lengthened southern platform of the original terminus, the outer end of which was used for MR departures and the inner for New Passage or, later, South Wales trains. Platform 7 was for arriving and departing Clifton Down and Avonmouth trains. Refreshment rooms were built in the apex between the old and new stations.

Even before its completion the station was inadequate, several minor accidents between 1871 and 1876 being attributed by Board of Trade inspectors directly or indirectly to the congested state of the new station. One report made in 1876, two years before official completion, asserted 'the station is clearly much less than adequate for the amount of traffic to be handled.' The bridge over the New Cut was widened so that the down platform could be lengthened and a down bay brought into use in October 1892, the narrowing of the gauge allowing an additional island platform six years later. In 1902 a wooden footbridge was built in the terminal station spoiling the vista of Brunel's roof, but was removed in the 1930s. In 1914 the GWR decided to remodel the permanent way, extend the station and install modern labour saving signalling, but the outbreak of World War 1 prevented these plans from going ahead.

By the 1920s traffic had grown to such an extent that on Bank Holidays trains were held in block from Highbridge waiting for a platform at Bristol and often had to stand outside Temple Meads for an hour. On summer

Top: **Temple Meads c1900.**
M.J. Tozer collection

Above: **Wyatt's train shed, view up**
1907.   *GWR*

Right: **Down end of Temple Meads**
c1895, B&E carriage shed in distance.
H.C. Leat, Bristol Photographic Society,
per M.J. Tozer

Above: **Frontage of Temple Meads c1900.**   *J. J. Herd collection*

Right: **Plan of Temple Meads 1845 & 1935**

Saturdays between 1920 and 1930 it was not unknown for local trains from Bath and Radstock to take two hours or more for the last mile into the station and on at least one occasion, the time for the last mile was 3hr 20min. The railway could not be blamed for this state of affairs as the only room for extension was over Bristol Corporation's cattle market and to this the city council raised objections. The only immediate post-World War 1 improvement was doubling the width of the footbridge spanning the platforms of the through station and providing a new exit from it direct to the approach road. This work was completed on 10 July 1920. Then in 1929, as a measure to assist in easing the Depression, the government, rather on the style of the recent Job Creation Scheme, made loans to carry out large public works and it was agreed that the enlargement of Temple Meads would qualify. Under the direction of P.E. Culverhouse the station was enlarged to more than twice its size, the number of platforms being increased from 9 to 15, a large slice of the adjoining market being bought. The longest platform, Nos 9 & 10 combined and the tenth longest in the country, was 1,366ft in length compared with the previous longest of 920ft, the length of all the platforms totalling two miles. All main platforms were provided with refreshment and waiting rooms. Work began in November 1930, Shanks & McEwan of Glasgow being the main contractors for the station. The roofs of the new platforms were of the 'umbrella' or 'arcade' type, while the buildings were constructed of white or brown carrara glazed bricks on a grey concrete plinth. During the conversion of the old through station

when the two island platforms of the 1878 station were taken out to allow the old main up and down through platforms to be widened, both up and down traffic operated from the new platforms Nos 1-5 built on the site of the down approach road. The reconstructed old through platforms were opened on 25 March 1935, the job having taken more than two years. The completed station had five up and five down platforms, a bay for Portishead trains and four platforms in the old terminus. The enlarged Temple Meads was completed in December 1935 and became a 'closed' station. The booking office, given a modern cast iron and bronze front, was set back to give a spacious circulating area. Passengers gained their platform by a 300ft long and 30ft wide subway also giving access to hairdressing saloons and baths while parcels were carried in electric trolleys along a special subway connecting the parcels depot with all platforms. Electric lifts connected platforms to the subway. In three places scissors crossings were provided between the platform and adjacent through road so that two trains could be accommodated simultaneously along one platform face. Rather surprisingly gas lighting was used for the new platforms and remained in use until 1960 when it was replaced by fluorescent tubes. This in turn was superseded by high pressure sodium lighting

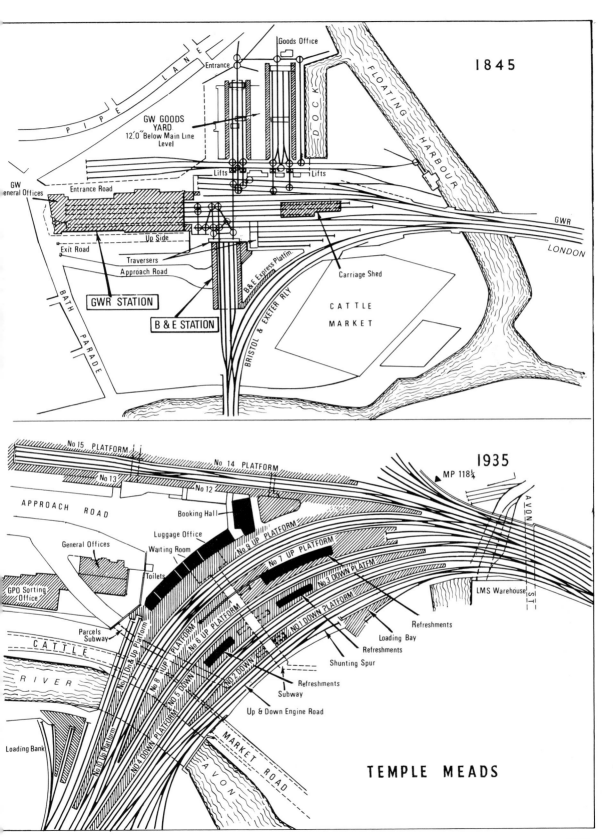

1845

PIPE LANE

Goods Office

Entrance

GW GOODS
YARD
12′0″ Below Main Line
Level

DOCK

FLOATING HARBOUR

Lifts

Lifts

GWR
LONDON

GW
General Offices

Entrance Road

Up Side

Exit Road

Traversers

Approach Road

GWR STATION

B & E STATION

B&E Express Platfm.

BATH PARADE

BRISTOL & EXETER RLY

Carriage Shed

CATTLE
MARKET

1935

No 15 PLATFORM

No 14 PLATFORM

No 13

No 12

MP 118¼

AVON

APPROACH ROAD

Booking Hall

Luggage Office

Waiting Room

No 9 UP PLATFORM

General Offices

Toilets

No 7 UP PLATFORM

No 3 DOWN PLATFM

LMS Warehouse

GPO Sorting
Office

No 1 DOWN PLATFORM

Refreshments

Parcels
Subway

CATTLE

No 11 Dn & Up Platform

No 8 UP PLATFORM

No 6 UP PLATFORM

No 5 DOWN

No 2 DOWN

Loading Bay

Refreshments

Shunting Spur

RIVER

No 4 DOWN PLATFORM

Refreshments

Subway

Up & Down Engine Road

Loading Bank

No 10 Up Platform

No 2 DOWN PLATFORM

AVON

MARKET ROAD

TEMPLE MEADS

103

Left: Francis Fox designed canopy, Temple Meads, 30 May 1980. *Author*

Centre left: View east from Temple Meads, 23 May 1933. To the left of coaches is the fish dock and to the right is the track bed for the station extension, while beyond is an LMS warehouse at Avonside Wharf. *GWR*

Bottom left: Work of extending Temple Meads. View west, 23 May 1933. Down bay platform on left. *GWR*

Right: View east from Pylle Hill, 23 May 1933. *GWR*

Below: The west end of Temple Meads, October 1935. *Veale & Co*

giving much better illumination and causing the number of cars stolen from the approach road to decrease by 50%. At the same time the tower was floodlit.

On 25 June 1940 Bristol had its first air raid, the prime target being Temple Meads since it was a key traffic centre. It received little damage, but on 2 December the station was hit and various suburban lines put out of action for several hours. On 6 December there were heavy casualties on the 7.10pm to Salisbury which received a direct hit at the station; the same day a bomb hit Bristol No 2 tunnel at St Anne's Park. On 3 January 1941 the station was the target for incendiary bombs and when all were thought to have been extinguished, one lodged behind the clock, started a fire which burnt out the booking offices – but passengers were soon buying tickets at army huts hurriedly erected in the station approach. The telegraph office, main refreshment room and clock tower were also burnt. Bristol was an important centre for both goods traffic and military personnel, wartime traffic often being hectic. Tunnels below the station were used as an emergency centre for key railwaymen and as an air raid shelter for passengers and staff. After cessation of hostilities, because the war had interfered with normal 'learn by experience' training of signal linesmen, from November 1946 the vault below Platform 9 was used as a technical school for a three months' intensive course in the installation and upkeep of mechanical and electrical signalling apparatus, points, track circuits and telephones.

With the contraction of passenger traffic in the 1960s, the platforms in Brunel's train shed, ironically known as the 'Midland station' because it was mostly used by LMR trains, became redundant, was closed 12 September 1965 and became a car park the following year. It is virtually the oldest surviving main line terminal station remaining in an almost unaltered state and is a Grade 1 listed building. At the time of writing, the Brunel Engineering Centre Trust has taken the lease of the original terminal buildings. To lessen the nuisance to passengers from starling and pigeon droppings in Wyatt's train shed, BR placed a contract in 1969 with Rentokil Laboratories to install nets over the eight louvres running the full 500ft length of the roof to block the gable ends from the 150ft high apex to just above vehicle roof level. It has proved successful, odd birds still enter, but not large flocks for roosting.

Parkway station opened on 1 May 1972 and has played its part in the continuing vitality of the railways in the Bristol area. Messrs Stone & Company won the contract for £50,000 of building a basic new station, car park and approach roads at Stoke Gifford on the site of the redundant marshalling yard. It was a great success as more than 1,000 passengers used it daily, the station proving particularly convenient to motorists living north of Bristol and wishing to use Inter-City trains, while motorists from the Bath area wishing to travel north can drive to the station, use the free car park and catch a train from there, a rather speedier way than changing at

Above left: Brown and cream tiled name in mid-1930s style and modern enamelled black and white sign, 30 May 1980. *Author*

Above: Blitzed coaches outside Temple Meads. *BR*

Right: Brunel's train shed, 9 October 1965. *Author*

Above left: Detail of pillar on Platform 3, 1 August 1980. *Author*

Far left: Corner of Merchantman buffet and bar, 30 May 1980. *Author*

Left: Entrance to platforms, Temple Meads, 1 August 1980. *Author*

Above: Temple Meads from west, 21 August 1980. *Author*

Right: Cleaning bird droppings from seat, 30 May 1980. *Author*

Temple Meads. As Parkway proved a success, its facilities were improved two years later when platform canopies and a full covering to the footbridge were provided.

Clifton Down station was most imposing in its heyday. In modified Gothic style, it had a superb mansion-like booking hall with a huge fireplace at either end. The platforms were formerly spanned by a ridge and furrow roof with fluted glass. It still retains double track as it is the passing station on the single line between Stapleton Road and Avonmouth Dock. Hotwells, the terminus of the Bristol Port Railway was situated in a cramped position in the Avon Gorge almost immediately below Clifton Suspension Bridge. The three roads were connected by a turntable. In its latter days, to obtain maximum use of the 280ft long platform, the locomotive stopped just short of the crossover which replaced the turntable, uncoupled, moved over to the parallel road where a wire hawser with a hook at each end was linked between the drawbar of the engine and a coach axle. The driver then drew forward gently pulling the train of about six four-wheeled

Top: The completed Bristol Parkway station, in April 1970 prior to opening.   *BR*

Above: A busy scene at Bristol Parkway.   *BR*

Right: Bristol Parkway: a general view taken in March 1974 showing the new weather canopies which cover much of the length of the two platforms and the covered footbridge which links with the waiting area and ticket office.   *BR*

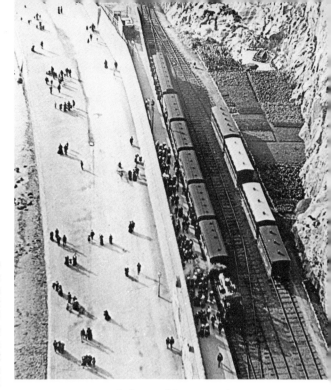

coaches into the station, the guard applying the brake as his van approached the platform. The two storey stone building was at the terminal end of the platform, trains being on a level with the upper storey and until 1893 it had a refreshment room. Hotwells closed on 19 September 1921 when the line was cut back to Hotwells Extension Platform which had opened 14 May 1917 as a wartime expedient so that workmen's trains of eight bogies could be handled. The Extension Platform was closed on 3 July 1922 as the site of the BPRP to Sneyd Park Junction was required for a new road to Avonmouth.

Ashton Gate Platform on the Portishead branch has had an interesting history. A simple wooden structure, it opened for football traffic only on 15 September 1906, closed towards the end of World War 1 and reopened 23 May 1926. Close to Bristol City Football Ground, at times it received through specials from the SR drawn by Pacifics and when football traffic was heavy, permission was given for an up train to be started from the down platform under supervision of an inspector and with a groundsman at the crossover points to clip them for the passage of the train. Closed on 7 September 1964, it was reopened to football specials, the first train to use it after reopening being a special three-car dmu from Birmingham on 29 September 1970. Since 1977 control problems have led to its disuse, Parson Street has been used instead. Because Temple Meads was unable to cope with any more trains, St Philip's was opened 2 May 1870, a timber built terminal station of one platform covered by a ridge and furrow glass roof. In the rationalisation following the enlargement of Temple Meads in the 1930s, it closed 21 September 1953.

Temple Meads goods yard was situated at right angles to the passenger terminus and 12ft below, access being by turntables and two hydraulically powered lifts acting rather like a pair of scales, each lowering a wagon and at the same time raising another, the operation taking about half a minute. The goods shed, 326ft by 138ft, was equipped with cranes for loading and unloading wagons, the depot holding 209. The shed was an example of Brunel's functional design at its best. It had a central span of 60ft plus two side spans of 40ft each. Columns were placed at 35ft centres along the building and longitudinal

trusses were provided in addition to the transverse trusses. Both sets used timber members in compression with wrought iron ties. The combination of solid-looking timbers and light metal ties, created a roof both functional and elegant. Hydraulic capstans and horses were used for wagon movements within the shed, Brunel remarking, 'We have several small capstan heads in different parts of the station, which are always in motion running round and a porter takes a turn round one of these with a rope which is hooked on to any carriage which he wishes to move.' In 1844 the GWR had six trains using the shed. An up GWR goods arrived at 7.30pm and the Bristol & Gloucester goods had to leave before it arrived, which meant that the BGR closed its doors at 5pm; even then, 2½hr was insufficient time to complete loading and invoicing. Competitive road transport accepted goods until 4pm and arrived in Gloucester for next morning's delivery, so the railway had but little advantage, yet its host, the GWR, did not close until 8pm and more goods were sent in between 5pm and 8pm than during the rest of the day. The shed handled B&E traffic until 1 May 1850 when its own shed was opened at Pylle Hill. The GWR depot was also used by the MR when that company took over the Bristol & Gloucester, narrow gauge rails having to be laid in 1854. The depot was inadequate to deal with the requirements of expanding traffic, so between 1874 and 1876 it was remodelled. Rowland Brotherhood of Chippenham obtained the contract. To give extra space, the old dock he had constructed about 35 years before which gave barges access to the Floating Harbour, was filled up and replaced by a new barge wharf with steam and hydraulic cranes. The whole surface of the goods yard was then raised 3ft 6in and the layout rearranged, the new shed

Above: Bristol-Portishead dmu and Portishead-Bristol passenger train hauled by Standard 2-6-2T No 82037 passing at Ashton Gate Platform, 7 June 1960. *R.E. Toop*

Above right: Ivatt 2-6-2T No 41240 leaving St Philip's with Bath train c1950. *Lens of Sutton*

Right: Fishponds, a Bristol suburban station on the MR c1910. *Author's collection*

having six platforms averaging 445ft in length and accommodation for 200 wagons with another 232 in the open yard. As delays caused by the lifts were unacceptable, an incline was built to the lower level so that a locomotive could shunt trucks to and from the depot; this 1 in 60 gradient assisted shunting as it made a natural hump yard. As the volume of traffic flowing into Bristol was much smaller than that outwards, No 1 platform was used for unloading and the other five for loading, except No 2 which was used until 9am for unloading inwards London goods. Wagons received on the two inwards berths could be shunted round when empty to the outwards loading roads by capstan and horse power without interfering with either the unloading operations, or the shunting work at the other end of the yard. All trains and engines to and from the main lines had to work over a short section of single line; at times this certainly mitigated against punctual working. By 1914 1,600-1,700 wagons went in and out of the depot daily, this figure including those for Redcliff Sidings. These sidings were an offshoot of Temple Meads where mineral, flour and grain traffic was accommodated; Temple Meads itself was confined to general goods except for consignments of galvanised iron which were loaded at the waterside. Nineteen trains conveying 600 wagons were despatched between 6pm and 6am.

To meet the demands of trade, in 1924 the GWR built a new depot and sidings involving an expenditure of

£556,450. To give sufficient area, dilapidated property between Victoria Street and Temple Back was bought. Covering an area of more than five acres, 15 platforms were under one roof, each pair of platforms 30ft wide and 575ft in length and connected to adjoining ones by means of tip-up balance bridges to facilitate trolleying. Unlike the old shed, each road had a platform. The new depot could accommodate 408 wagons under cover and 330 in the yard. Electric power was used extensively – electric points, electric capstans to move wagons and electric runways to expedite the conveyance of documents between the office and shed. Goods were carried by electric platform trucks and an electric telpher could convey up to a ton of goods to any part of the shed. A special carriage chute for dealing with cars, furniture vans and other road vehicles before and after rail conveyance was worked by an electric capstan. Electric

Above left: GWR goods shed, Bristol.   *J. C. Bourne*

Left: Former Temple Meads goods depot, now an NCL depot, 29 May 1980.   *Author*

Above: St Philip's goods station, 30 May 1922.   *NRM*

lifts served the cellarage (390ft by 100ft) and overhead warehouse. The cellarage was important to satisfy the ever increasing demand at the port for the storage of butter, cheese, lard, bacon and other perishables. In 1934 the depot dealt with over 4 million parcels and 1.5 million tons of goods.

The warehouse and goods shed at Canon's Marsh were opened in October 1906. 540ft by 133ft, it was of ferro-concrete on the Hennebique principle, there being 274 ferro-concrete piles averaging 32ft in depth in the foundations as the ground was soft. 35ft high, it had a floor area of 35,600sq ft. The steel and corrugated iron roof had Rendle's patent glazing. The contractor for the building was Robertson of Bristol. Four roads holding about 97 wagons passed through the building, with a platform 20ft wide between the two most northern lines and one of the same dimensions between the southern line and cartway. The depot was equipped with eight electric cranes and three 30cwt electric hoists. The 22 sidings in the yard accommodated 531 wagons. The upper storey of the shed was a warehouse. The depot was important as it gave rail access to the city docks and avoided the extra expense involved in carting or barging and relieved pressure on the two oldest depots in the city – Temple Meads and Pylle Hill. Later, increased warehouse accommodation to the extent of over 4,000sq yd was erected at Pylle Hill and new mileage depots were built at St Philip's Marsh and Stapleton Road.

Prior to 1858 the inwards and outwards goods departments of the MR at Bristol were carried on in the GWR's Temple Meads goods depot, but that year, because of an increase in traffic, the MR inwards goods department moved to the MR coal yard at St Philip's where a goods depot was erected and eight years later was doubled in size to accommodate the outwards department as well. The building erected by Humphries of Derby measured 180ft by 133ft and was supported on cast iron columns resting on wrought iron girders. Fifteen hydraulic cranes of Sir William Armstrong's patent pattern lifted up to two tons and were so placed that as one lifted goods from the trucks to the platform, another lifted goods from the platform to the trucks on the other side. Six traversing tables were worked by hydraulic power. Hydraulic capstan engines capable of moving 80 tons drew wagons in or out of the shed. Hydraulic power came from an Armstrong patent accumulator worked by two engines of about 60hp. A feature of the shed adopted from St Pancras passenger station was that below was spacious cellarage for the storage of over

15,000 hogsheads of Burton and other ales consigned to tradesmen in the neighbourhood, a new facility which the company had recently developed. The building also stabled 50 horses belonging to the MR while nearby were the corn lofts. The yard had 20 roads. A carriage dock permitted horse drawn furniture vans and other wheeled vehicles being loaded and discharged and extensive cattle pens and coal yards adjoined. Access to the goods station and the nearby St Philip's passenger station was by a single line to each. Through the years the shed received improvements, electric cranes supplementing those of the hydraulic pattern, but with a reduction in goods traffic, the depot, which had been renamed Bristol, Midland Road on 15 September 1952, closed on 1 April 1967.

Below: **Cattle dock and carriage sheds, St Philip's, 30 May 1922.** *NRM*

Locomotive Allocations

Bath Road and St Philip's Marsh Allocation 1914

0-6-0 Standard Goods
238, 504, 674, 792, 886, 1112, 1196, 1205, 1209.

2-4-0T Metro
459, 624, 632, 979, 1456.

0-4-2T '517' class
519, 528, 537, 539, 553, 599, 837, 846.

2-4-0 '806' class
823.

0-6-0ST/PT '850' class
989 PT, 1224 ST, 1916 PT, 1919 PT, 1928 PT, 1946 ST, 1952 ST, 1954 PT, 1964 ST, 1978 ST, 1995 PT, 1996 PT, 1998 PT, 2012 PT, 2015 ST, 2017 ST.

0-6-0ST '1076' class
1271, 1589, 1601.

0-6-0ST/PT '1854' class
1712 PT, 1719 PT, 1761 ST, 1794 PT, 1864 PT, 1877 PT, 1889 PT, 1893 ST, 1899 PT.

0-6-0ST '655' class
1746.

0-6-0ST '1813' class
1852.

0-6-0ST/PT '2021' class
2031 ST, 2035 ST, 2044 ST, 2059 ST, 2102 PT, 2115 PT, 2127 ST, 2130 PT, 2158 ST.

2-4-0T '2201' class
2201.

0-6-0 Dean Goods
2304, 2308, 2320, 2382, 2383, 2389, 2392, 2395, 2396, 2411, 2415, 2421-23, 2435, 2440, 2461, 2470, 2481, 2485, 2520, 2526, 2533, 2543, 2547, 2551, 2557, 2565, 2580.

0-6-0 '2361' class
2369, 2370, 2376, 2378.

2-6-0 Aberdare
2622, 2648.

0-6-0ST/PT '2721' class
2729 ST, 2761 PT, 2776 ST, 2786 ST, 2793 PT.

2-8-0 '2800' class
2809, 2821, 2828, 2854.

4-6-0 'Saint' class
2900 *William Dean*, 2922 *Saint Gabriel*, 2930 *Saint Vincent*, 2946 *Langford Court*, 2971 *Albion*, 2973 *Robins Bolitho*, 2974 *Lord Barrymore*, 2976 *Winterstoke*, 2982 *Lalla Rookh*, 2983 *Red Gauntlet*, 2985 *Peveril of the Peak*, 2986 *Robin Hood*, 2987 *Bride of Lammermoor*, 2990 *Waverley*.

2-6-2T '3150' class
3159, 3168.

2-4-0 '3201' class
3201

2-4-0 '3226' class
3231.

4-4-0 'Duke' class
3254 *Boscawen*, 3268 *River Tamar*.

4-4-0 'Atbara' class
3387 *Roberts*, 4136 *Terrible*, 4144 *Colombo*, 4145 *Dunedin*.

4-4-0 '3521' class
3533.

4-4-0 'City' class
3708 *Killarney*, 3715 *City of Hereford*, 3717 *City of Truro*.

4-4-0 'County' class
3802 *County Clare*, 3807 *County Kilkenny*, 3815 *County of Hants*, 3824 *County of Cornwall*, 3832 *County of Wilts*, 3833 *County of Dorset*.

4-4-0 'Badminton' class
4114 *Shelburne.*

4-4-0 'Flower' class
4153 *Camellia,* 4160 *Carnation,* 4164 *Mignonette,* 4166 *Polyanthus.*

2-6-0 '4300' class
4323, 4324, 4334, 4339.

Total 150

Bath Road Allocation 8 January 1938

0-6-0 PT '2021' class
2031.

0-6-0 Dean Goods
2485, 2568.

4-6-0 'Saint' class
2913 *Saint Andrew,* 2933 *Bibury Court,* 2934 *Butleigh Court,* 2936 *Cefntilla Court,* 2942 *Fawley Court,* 2943 *Hampton Court,* 2953 *Titley Court,* 2954 *Tockenham Court,* 2955 *Tortworth Court.*

4-4-0 'Bulldog' class
3308, 3330 *Orion,* 3363 *Alfred Baldwin,* 3370 *Sir John*

Llewelyn, 3371 *Sir Massey Lopes,* 3376 *River Plym,* 3380 *River Yealm,* 3396 *Natal Colony.*

4-6-0 'Star' class
4019 *Knight Templar,* 4022 *Belgian Monarch,* 4033 *Queen Victoria,* 4035 *Queen Charlotte,* 4041 *Prince of Wales,* 4042 *Prince Albert,* 4043 *Prince Henry,* 4055 *Princess Sophia,* 4057 *Princess Elizabeth,* 4062 *Malmesbury Abbey,* 4069 *Westminster Abbey,* 4071 *Cleeve Abbey.*

Below: No 5506 still lettered 'GWR' stands outside Bath Road depot, 19 August 1951.   *H. Ballantyne*

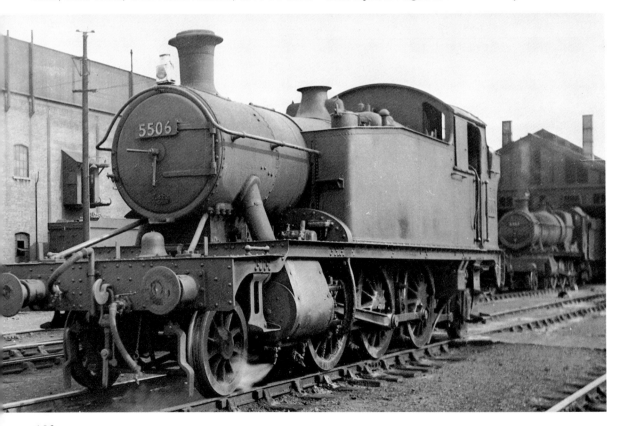

4-6-0 'Castle' class
4016 *Knight of the Golden Fleece*, 4081 *Warwick Castle*, 4082 *Windsor Castle*, 4096 *Highclere Castle*, 5025 *Chirk Castle*, 5048 *Earl of Devon*, 5084 *Reading Abbey*.

2-6-0 '4300' class
4371, 4394, 5306, 6340, 6368, 7307.

2-6-2T '5400' class
4507, 4508, 4535, 4551, 4562, 4563, 4566, 4568, 4572, 4573, 4577, 4580, 4585, 4588, 4592, 5506-08, 5510, 5512, 5514, 5523, 5528, 5535, 5536, 5540,

5541, 5547, 5548, 5553-56, 5558, 5560, 5562-64, 5566.

4-6-0 'Hall' class
4923, *Evenley Hall*, 4945 *Milligan Hall*, 4949 *Packwood Hall*, 5969 *Honington Hall*.

2-6-2T '5100' class
5158, 5169.

Total 90

St Philip's Marsh Allocation 8 January 1938

2-4-0T Metro
1497.

0-6-0PT '1501' class
1542.

0-6-0PT '850' class
1945, 1964, 2013, 2015.

0-6-0PT '2021' class
2044, 2070, 2072.

0-6-0 '2251' class
2251-53, 2258, 2260, 2265, 2269, 2277.

0-6-0 Dean Goods
2340, 2381, 2426, 2445, 2454, 2461, 2467, 2526, 2528, 2534, 2564, 2567, 2573.

0-6-0 '2361' class
2362.

2-8-0 '2800' class
2806, 2834, 2851, 2859.

2-8-0 ROD class
3013, 3019, 3035, 3041, 3045.

4-4-0 'Bulldog' class
3378 *River Tawe*.

0-6-0PT '8750' class
3720, 3731, 3733, 3759, 3763, 8779, 8793, 8795, 9721, 9729, 9733, 9764, 9771-73, 9784.

2-8-0T '4200' class
4221.

0-4-2T '4800' class
4836, 4854, 4855.

4-6-0 'Hall' class
4925 *Eynsham Hall*, 4956 *Plowden Hall*, 4959 *Purley Hall*, 4963 *Rignall Hall*, 4964 *Rodwell Hall*, 4969 *Shrugborough Hall*, 4986 *Aston Hall*, 4992 *Crosby Hall*, 5900 *Hinderton Hall*, 5911 *Preston Hall*, 5943 *Elmdon Hall*.

2-6-2T '5101' class
5110.

2-6-2T '5100' class
5118, 5126.

0-6-0PT '5700' class
5770, 5771, 5781, 5784, 5785, 7718, 7719, 7726, 7728, 7729, 7779, 7782, 7784, 7790, 7792-95, 8702, 8703, 8713, 8722, 8730, 8737, 8741.

0-4-2 '5800' class
5803, 5806, 5809.

2-6-0 '4300' class
6303, 6314, 6322, 6360, 7302, 7312, 7316, 8308, 8314, 8320.

0-6-2T '5600' class
6600.

4-6-0 'Grange' class
6804 *Brockington Grange*, 6836 *Estevarney Grange*, 6842 *Nunhold Grange*, 6859 *Yiewsley Grange*.

Total 118

Bath Road Allocation 27 February 1954

4-6-0 'County' class
1005 *County of Devon*, 1007 *County of Brecknock*, 1011 *County of Chester*, 1014 *County of Glamorgan*, 1026 *County of Salop*, 1028 *County of Warwick*.

0-4-2T '1400' class
1415, 1430, 1454, 1463.

4-6-0 'Star' class
4056 *Princess Margaret*.

4-6-0 'Castle' class
4073 *Caerphilly Castle*, 4075 *Cardiff Castle*, 4084 *Aberystwyth Castle*, 4091 *Dudley Castle*, 4094 *Dynevor Castle*, 4096 *Highclere Castle*, 5000 *Launceston Castle*, 5019 *Treago Castle*, 5025 *Chirk Castle*, 5037 *Monmouth Castle*, 5048 *Earl of Devon*, 5064 *Bishop's Castle*, 5067 *St Fagans Castle*, 5069 *Isambard Kingdom Brunel*, 5074 *Hampden*, 5076 *Gladiator*, 5085 *Evesham Abbey*, 5094 *Tretower Castle*, 5096 *Bridgwater Castle*, 7011 *Banbury Castle*, 7014 *Caerhays Castle*, 7019 *Fowey Castle*, 7034 *Ince Castle*.

2-6-2T '5101' class
4139, 4157, 4159, 4166, 5182, 5197.

2-6-2T '4500' class
4532, 4535, 4558, 4577, 4582, 4592, 4595, 4597, 5506, 5512, 5514, 5523, 5525, 5528, 5532, 5535, 5546-48, 5553, 5559, 5561, 5565.

0-6-0PT '8750' class
4603, 4660, 9604, 9610.

4-6-0 'Hall' class
4909 *Blakesley Hall*, 4942 *Maindy Hall*, 4961 *Pyrland Hall*, 5904 *Kelham Hall*, 5919 *Worlsey Hall*, 5949 *Trematon Hall*, 6900 *Abney Hall*, 6972 *Beningbrough Hall*, 6977 *Grundisburgh Hall*, 6981 *Marbury Hall*, 6982 *Melmerby Hall*, 6997 *Bryn-Ivor Hall*, 7901 *Dodington Hall*, 7907 *Hart Hall*.

2-6-0 '4300' class
5307, 6451.

0-4-2T '5800' class
5809, 5813.

2-6-2T '6100' class
6107.

4-6-0 'Grange' class
6867 *Peterston Grange*.

0-6-0PT '5700' class
7782.

4-4-0 'Earl' class
9016, 9020, 9026.

Total 91

St Philip's Marsh Allocation 27 February 1954

0-6-0PT '1600' class
1649.

0-6-0PT '2021' class
2053, 2070, 2072.

0-6-0 '2251' class
2203, 2215, 2250, 2251, 2261, 2265, 2269, 2293, 3215.

0-6-0 Dean Goods
2411.

2-8-0 '2800' class
2845, 2846, 2879, 2889, 2898, 3854.

2-8-0 ROD class
3014, 3017, 3032.

0-6-0PT '8750' class
3604, 3614, 3623, 3632, 3643, 3676, 3720, 3731, 3748, 3758, 3759, 3763-65, 3773, 3784, 3795, 4619, 4624, 4626, 4655, 4688, 8790, 8795, 9605, 9606, 9626, 9729, 9771.

2-8-0T '4200' class
4262.

2-8-0 '4700' class
4703, 4706.

4-6-0 'Hall' class
4914, *Cranmore Hall*, 4947 *Nanhoran Hall*, 4958 *Priory Hall*, 4983 *Albert Hall*, 4999 *Gopsal Hall*, 5924 *Dinton Hall*, 5982 *Harrington Hall*, 6908 *Downham Hall*, 6925 *Hackness Hall*, 6936 *Breccles Hall*, 6954 *Lotherton Hall*, 6957 *Norcliffe Hall*, 6958 *Oxburgh Hall*, 6986 *Rydal Hall*, 7908 *Henshall Hall*.

2-6-0 '4300' class
5306, 5325, 5350, 5351, 5367, 6322, 6363, 6370, 6374, 7303.

0-6-2T '5600' class
5675, 6601, 6656, 6670, 6671.

0-6-0PT '5700' class
5784, 7718, 7719, 7728, 7729, 7749, 7780, 7783, 7790, 7793, 7795, 8702, 8703, 8713, 8714, 8722, 8730, 8737, 8741, 8746, 8747.

4-6-0 'Grange' class
6804 *Brockington Grange*, 6811 *Cranbourne Grange*, 6827 *Llanfrechfa Grange*, 6830 *Buckenhill Grange*, 6842 *Nunhold Grange*, 6845 *Paviland Grange*, 6846 *Ruckley Grange*, 6852 *Headbourne Grange*, 6863 *Dolhywel Grange*, 6876 *Kingsland Grange*.

2-8-2T '7200' class
7201, 7250.

0-6-0PT '9400' class
8413, 8491, 8492, 9453, 9481, 9488.

0-6-0DE Class 08
13000-13003.

0-6-0DE
15100, 15107.

2-6-0 Class 2MT
46525-27.

4-6-0 Class 5MT
73019, 73022, 73027-29, 73032, 73039.

2-8-0 Class WD
90176, 90251, 90284.

ex-GWR diesel railcars
23, 24, 28, 35, 36.

Total 143 plus 5 railcars

Barrow Road Allocation 1914

2-4-0 '1P' class
89, 90, 92, 104, 155, 178.

4-4-0 '2P' class
516-527.

4-2-2 '1P' class
607, 609, 614, 635-39, 643-45, 661-64, 669.

0-4-4T '1P' class
1228, 1331-39, 1388-90, 1397.

0-6-0T '1F' class
1870-74.

0-6-0 '1F' class
2363, 2490, 2606, 2608-10, 2632, 2665, 2724, 2829, 2833.

0-6-0 '2F' class
2988, 3071, 3072, 3074, 3076, 3077, 3079, 3087.

0-6-0 '3F' class
3155, 3156, 3159, 3193, 3194, 3400, 3593, 3594, 3615, 3621, 3712, 3713.

Total 84

Above: LMS 0-4-4T No 1337 shunting at Clifton Down in 1929. *G. Farr*

Barrow Road Allocation September 1935

2-4-0 '1P' class
157.

4-4-0 '2P' class
518, 520, 522-24, 629.

4-4-0 '4P' class
1023, 1025-28, 1030.

0-4-4T '1P' class
1228, 1267, 1334, 1337, 1338, 1364, 1389, 1391, 1397, 1404.

0-6-0T '1F' class
1706, 1815, 1870, 1874.

0-6-0 '2F' class
3071, 3154, 3173.

0-6-0 '3F' class
3178, 3180, 3181, 3186, 3419, 3436, 3439, 3444, 3464, 3593, 3712, 3727, 3729.

0-6-0 '4F' class
3840, 3873, 3875, 3876, 3908, 4122, 4134, 4135, 4169, 4170, 4273, 4276-78, 4424, 4533, 4534, 4535, 4536.

4-6-0 '5P5F' class
5043, 5044, 5066, 5094*-97

0-6-0T '3F' class
7316, 16761 (7678).

2-4-0 '1P' class
20092.

Total 72   * On loan

Barrow Road Allocation 30 January 1954

2-6-2T '3P' class
40116, 40120, 40164, 40174.

4-4-0 '2P' class
40426, 40486.

2-6-2T '2MT' class
41240.

0-6-0T '1F' class
41706.

0-6-0 '3F' class
43427, 43462, 43464, 43593, 43712, 43734.

0-6-0 '4F' class
43926, 43928, 43932, 43953, 44135, 44169, 44266, 44269, 44296, 44317, 44355, 44411, 44424, 44466, 44534, 44536, 44537, 44553, 44569.

4-6-9 '5MT' class
44743, 44745, 44747.

4-6-0 'Jubilee' class
45561 *Saskatchewan*, 45572 *Eire*, 45577 *Bengal*, 45602 *British Honduras*, 45651 *Shovell*, 45660 *Rooke*, 45662 *Kempenfelt*, 45663 *Jervis*, 45682 *Trafalgar*, 45685 *Barfleur*, 45690 *Leander*, 45699 *Galatea*.

0-6-0T '3F' class
47333, 47544, 47550, 47552, 47678.

0-4-0ST 'OF' class
51202, 51212.

Total 55

Below: 'Pug' No 51212 at Barrow Road MPD yard, 19 August 1951.   *H. Ballantyne*

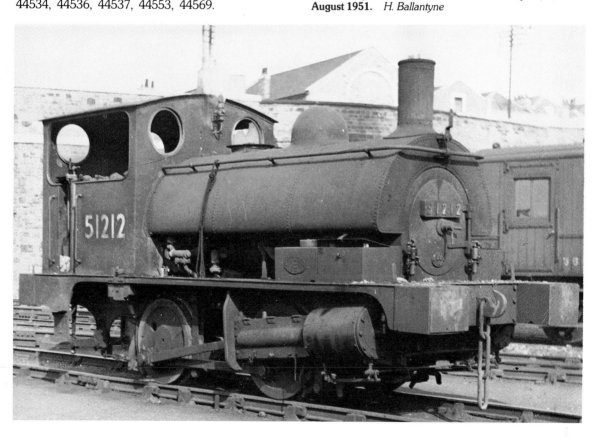

Bath Road Allocation 17 July 1980

Set No   *DMUs*

Class 101/2
805 50304 59122 50329
806 50319 59123 50335

Class 118/1
460 51302 59469 50317
462 51304 59471 51319
465 51307 59474 51322
466 51308 59475 51323
467 51309 59476 51324
468 51310 59477 51325
469 51311 59490 51326
471 51314 59481 51329
472 51315 59482 51530

Class 102
800 51445 59549 51515
801 51446 59547 51517
802 51449 59550 51521
803 51450 59546 51522
804 51452 59551 51523
812 51462 59530 51530
813 51463 59561 51533
822 51495 59096 51510
820 51500 59093 51512
823 51505 59082 51511
821 51509 59050 51513
811 51519 59548 51801
810 51799 59539 51808

Class 121
132 55032
133 55033

Bath Road MPD, 9 July 1960.
H. Ballantyne

Class 50 Co-Co
50.039-044

Class 31 A1A-A1A
31.118, 31.123, 31.128, 31.131, 31.136, 31.145, 31.154, 31.159, 31.165, 31.170, 31.210, 31.231, 31.258, 31.286, 31.294, 31.296, 31.307, 31.401, 31.419-424.

Class 47 Co-Co
47.001, 47.008, 47.020, 47.026, 47.032, 47.035, 47.083, 47.091, 47.095, 47.099, 47.101, 47.129, 47.136-138, 47.140, 47.142, 47.152, 47.159, 47.244-252, 47.267, 47.282-286, 47.293, 47.327.

Class 37 Co-Co
37.158, 37.159, 37.203-208, 37.210, 37.224, 37.231-233, 37.241, 37.295.

Class 03 0-6-0
03.121, 03.382.

Class 08 0-6-0
08.185, 08.218, 08.338, 08.363, 08.483, 08.491, 08.643, 08.668, 08.756, 08.800, 08.821, 08.900, 08.935, 08.942, 08.950, 08.951.

**Totals: 2 single car dmus
24 3-car dmus
99 locomotives**

Bibliography

Ahrons, E.L; *Locomotive & Train Working in the latter part of the Nineteenth Century: Vols 2 & 4;* Heffer 1952.

Allen, C. J; *Titled Trains of the Western;* Ian Allan Ltd, 1974.

Allen, G.F; *The Western Since 1948;* Ian Allan Ltd, 1979.

Arrowsmith, J.W; *Dictionary of Bristol;* Bristol, 1906.

Buchanan, R.A; Cossons, N; *The Industrial Archaeology of the Bristol Region;* David & Charles, 1969.

Clinker, C.R; *Closed Stations & Goods Depots;* Avon Anglia, 1978.

Clinker, C.R; 'Railway Development at Bristol', *Railway Magazine;* September, October, November 1956.

Cocks, R.H; 'Notable Railway Stations: Temple Meads,' *Railway Magazine;* October 1900.

Cooke, R.A; *Track Layout Diagrams of the GWR and BR WR Section 19;* Author 1975.

Cornock, W; 'Railway Warehouses and Goods Depots', *Railway & Travel Monthly;* June 1914.

Cullen, E; 'Industrial Development by Railways: Canon's Marsh Extension', *Great Western Railway Magazine;* June 1906.

Fellows, Canon R.B; 'Rival Routes to Bristol', *Railway World;* November/December 1960.

Fleming, D.J; *St Philip's Marsh;* Bradford Barton 1980.

Hateley, R; *Industrial Locomotives of South Western England;* Industrial Railway Society 1977.

Kichenside, G.M; 'WR's £4m Bristol Resignalling Plan', *Modern Railways;* July 1968.

Latimer, J; *Annals of Bristol in the Nineteenth Century;* Bristol, 1887.

Leleux, S.A; *Brotherhoods, Engineers;* David & Charles, 1965.

Lyons, E; *An Historical Survey of Great Western Engine Sheds 1947;* Oxford Publishing Co, 1972.

MacDermott, E.T./Clinker, C.R. and Nock, O.S; *History of the Great Western Railway;* Ian Allan Ltd, 1964/1967.

Maggs, C.G; *Bristol & Gloucester Railway;* Oakwood Press, 1969.

Maggs, C.G; *Bristol Port Railway & Pier;* Oakwood Press, 1975.

Maggs, C.G; 'The Railways between Bristol and Bath', *Railway World;* February, March, April 1960.

Neale, W.G; *At the Port of Bristol;* Port of Bristol Authority, 1970.

Nock, O.S; 'Resorts for Railfans, Bristol', *Trains Illustrated;* May 1952.

Pell-Hiley, A.G; 'Twenty Four Hours at Bristol', *Railway Magazine;* October 1909.

Railway Correspondence & Travel Society; *Locomotives of the Great Western Railway;* RCTS, 1952 -74.

Rust, C.R; 'A Stationmaster's Day at Bristol Temple Meads', *Railway Magazine;* September 1959.

Vaughan, A; *A Pictorial Record of Great Western Architecture;* Oxford Publishing Co, 1977.

Vaughan, A; *A Pictorial Record of Great Western Signalling;* Oxford Publishing Co, 1973.

Vincent, M; *Lines to Avonmouth;* Oxford Publishing Co, 1979.

Warnock, D.W; *The Bristol & North Somerset Railway 1863-1884;* Temple Cloud, 1978.

Warnock D.W. & Parsons, R.G; *The Bristol & North Somerset Railway Since 1884;* Avon Anglia, 1979.

Warburton, M.B; 'Serving the Port of Bristol', *Railway Magazine;* August 1972.

Whitley, H.S; 'The Canon's Marsh Extension, Bristol', *Great Western Railway Magazine;* July 1906.

Anon 'Avon Metro', *Modern Railways;* January 1980.

Anon 'Bristol as a Railway Centre', *Modern Transport;* May 1924.

Anon 'The Bristol Division of the Great Western Railway', *Railway Gazette;* May 1924.

Anon 'New Works at Bristol', *Engineer;* January 1907.

End papers: **Bristol MAS area**